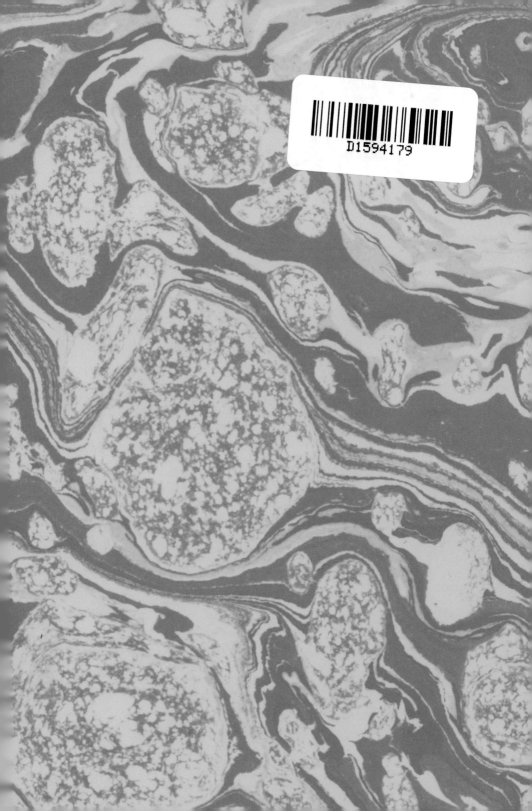
D1594179

INQUIRY INTO THE PICTURESQUE

SIDNEY K. ROBINSON

INQUIRY INTO THE PICTUR~ ESQUE

The University of Chicago Press   *Chicago & London*

SIDNEY K. ROBINSON is an architect and an associate professor in
the School of Architecture at the University of Illinois at Chicago.

The University of Chicago Press, Chicago 60637
The University of Chicago Press, Ltd., London

© 1991 by The University of Chicago
All rights reserved. Published 1991
Printed in the United States of America
00 99 98 97 96 95 94 93 92 91   5 4 3 2 1

Library of Congress Cataloging-in-Publication Data

Robinson, Sidney K., 1943–
    Inquiry into the picturesque / Sidney K. Robinson.
        p.   cm.
    Includes bibliographical references (p.   ).
    ISBN 0-226-72251-1
    1. Picturesque, The.   2. Aesthetics, British—18th century.
    3. Aesthetics, Modern   I. Title.
    BH211.P53R62   1991
    111'.85—dc20   90-20338

♾ The paper used in this publication meets the minimum requirements
of the American National Standard for Information Sciences—
Permanence of Paper for Printed Library Materials, ANSI Z39.48-1984.

Endpapers: "This is a motley emblem of my work": Tristram Shandy.
Front: *Tristram Shandy*, Laurence Sterne, London, Cadell & Davies, 1798
Back: *Tristram Shandy*, Laurence Sterne, London, Cadell & Davies, 1819

*To my mother, who gave me the love of words, and
to the memory of my father, who gave me the love of liberty*

Contents

Acknowledgments

This inquiry into the Picturesque has, as is appropriate, a number of origins and a number of sources. Over several years, colleagues have engaged me in stimulating and challenging discussions. I would like to acknowledge Allen Scult, rhetorician; Charles Hoch, planning theorist; Richard Guy Wilson, architectural historian. From their differing points of view they kept the perspective broad as well as penetrating.

The initial impulse to look at the Picturesque came from working with Alden B. Dow, whose studio and house are the most striking examples I know of this mode of composition. I will always be grateful for his inspiration.

My stay in England was made most comfortable by the charming hosts I enjoyed in Bath, Sue and Paul Hayward.

The encouragement to finish the work was given by Stanley Tigerman, director of the School of Architecture at the University of Illinois at Chicago. I appreciate his confidence and his insistence. Wendelin Mutch Arnold cleaned up the bibliography in exemplary fashion for which I am very grateful.

Iowa State University provided the support for the sabbatical semester in England, and the University of Illinois's award of a University Scholar Fellowship underwrote numerous activities.

Karen Wilson and Jean Eckenfels, editors, and Joan Sommers, designer, at the University of Chicago Press were unfailingly supportive and helpful.

Prologue

The Picturesque has undergone so many transformations since its initial discussion in eighteenth-century England that it is hard to say just what it is. It presumably has something to do with landscape scenes including trees, rocks, and water. These natural objects are not arranged to make a composition that is soft and smooth; neither is it grand and overpowering. The Picturesque lies on an irregular path somewhere in between. In addition to gardens and parks, buildings, towns, clothing, and food, among other things, can be arranged in this manner or seen in this way by a prepared observer.

These essays take up the Picturesque in its late eighteenth-century English phase and turn it various ways to pick out patterns that link it with other compositions whose haphazard appearance or lack of clearly systematic arrangement are, in fact, the result of conscious choices. Because the boundary of the Picturesque is an intricate one, there are many edges to make contact with associated compositions. A collection of essays, in addition to being characteristic of an older practice, allows a freely composed arrangement of Whigs and pastoral poetry as well as aspects of the Picturesque including mixture, artifice, and connection.

Dissatisfaction with a compositional mode that seeks seamless control over all constituent elements underlies the picturesque attitude. Mixture is employed to interrupt such an emerging domination and is one of two characteristics of the Picturesque presented here. The second characteristic is the use of less power than is available to compose the parts in an arrangement that does not press for a conclusion. To tolerate some irregularity, to risk withholding complete control means that the Picturesque depends on a preexisting condition of plenitude that can be spiritual or intellec-tual, as well as material. Whether a Japanese prince roughs it in a seaside hut, a Whig grandee calls for open discussion, or a British gentleman allows hedges to grow untrimmed or cottage walls to crack, they all create an ambiguous situation by not taking visible control in direct proportion to their resources. A contemporary expression of avoiding a full-bore display of control can be found in Italo Calvino when he says: "I am trying to employ a rule of discretion that consists in maintaining my position slightly below the narrative possibilities at my disposal. Which, if you look closer, is the sign of real wealth."

an associate view

The choice to live below one's means, at least intermittently, is comfortable only if there is little or no risk to one's place in the natural or social world. When you come upon the patterns resulting from that choice, you cannot be sure what you see. They may look irregular, even unkempt, but further inquiry reveals an organizing principle that withholds control as well as exercising it. Deciding whether one is being misled, entertained, or challenged is an inte-gral part of a picturesque experience.

1st essay

A boundary for this amorphous category can be defined by collecting examples of things called Picturesque. Such collections have provided rich sources of images serving as definitions by example. The goal of the present collection of essays is to explore the intricate boundary of the Picturesque rather than to erect a defensible perimeter. The Picturesque irritates obvious centers of organization with irregular skirmishes on the outskirts rather than overwhelming assaults on the geometric citadel.

what does he mean by boundary

In the intervening two hundred years since its initial discus-sion and in locations beyond England, the Picturesque has been altered and extended in many ways. Along the way it has acquired a pejorative tint. Because pictures are representations, they are removed one step from what is "real." For this reason they are considered unreliable and misleading when examining matters of substance. If pictures are removed from reality, then the Picturesque, being "like a picture," is removed an additional step and opens itself to attack for being a misrepresentation. Arranging substantial things like trees and rocks and water to look like a picture can be construed as a dangerous deception. Partial concealment produces uncertainty.

The Picturesque has also been relegated to a diminutive status. Its weakness and charm can be used as superficial flourishes added to substantial meaning. Diversion or entertainment becomes its only recognized function. Serious people do not linger long in a picturesque world. Like the pastoral, it is a slender reed that bends rather than supports.

Wandering and searching are essentially picturesque activities that the eighteenth century formalized for tourists traveling to views recognized as pictures. Scenes could be collected by travelers who gave the views a status removed from the "original" meaning given them by local inhabitants.

A return to the commentaries of Richard Payne Knight, Uvedale Price, and others could be directed toward establishing the essence of the Picturesque. These rereadings are not a search for an original definition. In addition to visiting gardens and geologic locations associated with the Picturesque in the eighteenth century, looking again at these texts reminds us how complex and intriguing the early statements were. The intention here is to stimulate vigilant skepticism by roughing up the smooth banality of current usage. Such destabilization is encouraged because centralized compositions claim a survival value in the pursuit of a stable identity. They require continuous challenge to avoid becoming unresponsively despotic.

The work on the Picturesque that has already been done is significant in giving us a clearer picture of the images and forms associated with this pervasive aesthetic mode. Christopher Hussey takes first place with his 1927 book *The Picturesque: Studies in a Point of View*. David Watkin's *English Vision*, of 1982, is the most comprehensive recent example. The present collection of essays is not a revisionist history with the goal of "getting it right," at last, but the encouragement of a growth that defenders of obvious systems may consider needs trimming rather than cultivation.

The absence of pictures in this volume may need some comment. Etchings and photographs (black and white and, more seriously, color) give a sense of material reality that can only distract from these comments, which are not about arranging materials, whether trees or stones, into patterns we can call Picturesque. The subject here is how things are composed beyond the retina. Because pictures seem to assure congruence between mind and eye, their absence allows certain questions to be posed. To what extent the Picturesque is a visual category is one of the questions raised here. Visibility would appear to be the key to a category with such a name, but the Picturesque, rather than ratifying visibility, shows us how unreliable it ultimately is. The doubt that "what you see may not be what you get" initiates a search for the structure of power implicating the viewer as well as organizing the composition being viewed.

Each one of the following essays is spotted with implied ellipses. Conclusions are often left to the reader. This partial concealment of possible implications is part of the picturesque mode and comes naturally to the author whose training as an architect prepared him to seek out materials for new compositions, rather than simply to enjoy the contemplation of a completed whole. Whether the compositional mode employed is smoothness masquerading as roughness or roughness passing as smoothness is left to the reader to decide.

MIXTURE

As a young man Uvedale Price, who with Richard Payne Knight became the most outspoken advocate for the Picturesque in the late eighteenth century, was asked to improve an "old-fashioned" garden. His improvement completely replaced the "old" with the "modern." When he recounted this event in his essay *On the Picturesque* (1794), he regretted his rash destruction of the existing pattern. "I could have made use of it mixed with the modern style," he lamented. By the time Price wrote his book, the Picturesque was no longer just "the modern style." He had come to understand it as an attitude that mixed contrasting patterns. In a later edition of his essay (1842), Price included a similar story about Richard Payne Knight's consultation with the owner of Powis Castle over the systematic destruction of an uneven stretch of ground to make a smooth, green lawn. Knight, however, had no need for regret because he successfully persuaded the gentleman not to blow up the rocks, but to accept the roughness instead.

Price's confession of error establishes mixture as a central feature of the Picturesque. A composition that searches out contrast departs significantly from a more traditional ideal of coherence achieved by a thoroughgoing exclusion of nonconforming features. The ideals associated with Price's recommendation of mixture and its implications are the subject of the following comments.

Price describes the kind of picturesque composition he had in mind as having "no distinct lines of separation; all is mixed and blended together." But having said that, he goes on to identify the opposite condition of "abrupt variation" between the parts as characteristic of the Picturesque. Somehow the distinct characters of the parts are not compromised even when they "are perpetually mixed together." Their independent natures are not easily separated, but they are somehow separable. What was to be mixed, in what proportions, and to what degree constitute a large part of the controversy over aesthetic and political compositions that appeared in books and magazine articles in the latter part of the eighteenth century.

Time's accumulations and changes are the model for the kind of mixture the Picturesque advocates. When Knight applies the Picturesque to architecture, he recommends a "mixed style, . . . built piece-meal, during successive ages; and by several different nations. It is distinguished by no particular manner of execution, or class of ornaments, but admits of all promiscuously." Both the strength and the vulnerability of the Picturesque stem from its promiscuity. By avoiding a fixed system of rules, picturesque compositions can change and adjust to different conditions. Conversely, by embracing permissive habits in making choices, such compositions run the risk of disappearing into a random background.

The concentrated energy of an assertion competing with other assertions or standing out against a background of diffused energy is an unmistakable desire for identity. The Picturesque is certainly an assertion in these terms. It makes sense only against a background that allows its pattern to be identified even if preservation of that identity requires constant adjustment. A paradox lies in the assertion of promiscuity, which, fully carried out, can result in self-destruction. Much of the obscurity and apparent contradiction mixed into the discussion of the Picturesque originates in this problem of identity.

Time's changing effects are noticed when compared with a previous state of organization. An initial expenditure of organized energy must precede any subsequent satisfaction taken with time's inroads. In his visit to Italy, Price delighted in the "old" gardens whose original symmetry had been obscured. The satisfying mix-

2

ture of order and unconstrained growth was based on the obvious
structure of Renaissance gardens that held the variety of neglect in
place. Two kinds of formality, one good because it is disguised and
one bad because it is bald, need to be distinguished in order to
admit some of it into a picturesque composition. "There is a wide
difference between an avowed and characteristic formality, and a
formality, not less real, but which assumes the airs of ease and
playfulness." Assuming airs of playfulness is a neat summary of the
problem of trying to determine the identity of the Picturesque.

The English taste for gardens and parks that were not entirely
arranged according to some geometrical system developed in the
early years of the eighteenth century. The names of Joseph Addison, Lord Burlington, and Alexander Pope among others have been
placed at the head of a list of gentlemen advocating some degree of
"naturalness" in garden art. Determining what exactly is "natural"
initiated a discussion that has not reached an easy conclusion. In
very abbreviated terms, the controversy focused on the degree to
which human artifice should be aligned with either nature's appearance or its invisible laws. The Picturesque tried to occupy a shifting
position that mixed an obvious and conventionally geometric artifice with an irregular, less apparent artifice derived from nature.
Nature's appearance was a reference, but the designer maintained
his liberty to arrange trees, water, and rocks according to a compositional ideal.

Looked at in a casual way, botanical and geological nature
present a variety of forms, colors, and textures. They grow and
change. Compared to human ideals, nature appears to deviate from
any obvious rule. By choosing to make mixture a salient feature of
its aesthetic recommendations, the Picturesque admitted into its
compositions sensory stimuli that would traditionally have been
excluded because of the confusion they were thought to produce in
the pursuit of an idealized nature.

The Picturesque used nature deceptively according to some
because, although it referred to nature, it was not obedient. Those

3

who appealed to "nature" for an authentic set of relationships to guide human constructions did so either to justify their present, usually dominant, relationship with nature and society or to escape the continual questioning of the relation between nature and artifice that picturesque mixture requires.

Joseph Addison's *Spectator* essays from June and July 1712 introduced a more inclusive aesthetic perception. In these essays he combined a growing interest in the "rough, careless strokes of Nature" with the traditional "nice Touches and Embellishments of Art." His discovery of a new delight "when Chance seems to have the Effect of Design" is an early stage in the development of what might be called a theory of aesthetic composition. Serious consideration of things rough and careless in aesthetic matters generated complex implications that may surprise those who usually think of the Picturesque as a way to dismiss superficial work.

Another early advocate of more natural gardens was Robert Castell, whose *Villas of the Ancients*, published in 1728 and dedicated to Lord Burlington, identified three stages in the development of the Roman garden. The first stage was rough and naive. The second was arranged by rule and line. The third was a "close Imitation of Nature; where tho' the Parts are disposed with the greatest Art, the Irregularity is still preserved; so that their manner can not improperly be said to be an artful Confusion, where there is no Appearance of that Skill which is made use of, their Rocks, Cascades, and Trees, bearing their natural forms." The first two stages can be clearly stated in direct terms. The third, however, requires modifications and exceptions. The use of "tho'" and "still" and "not improperly" alerts us that we are in the presence of something whose appearance is not sufficient to its understanding. This third stage directs attention away from human activity by having it assume a "natural form." Castell's sequence recognizes that the acquisition and exercise of control finally reach a point of assurance and reflective self-consciousness that chooses to represent an earlier stage, whether from nostalgia or from a newly acquired sophistication.

china affects cottage too

An association with China was one of the more striking supports for this mixed form of garden design. Responding to the views of Chinese gardens brought to Europe by Fra Matteo Ripa in 1724, the likes of Lord Burlington and Sir William Chambers, who himself had been to China, linked Republican Rome to Confucian China not only through their garden art, but through their political morality. They recognized that a new composition whose parts were freed from the absolute alignment like iron filings tyrannized by a magnet satisfied their desire for a just balance between individual citizens and the nation as well as a harmonious combination of human artifice arranging natural features.

Mixture begins by identifying elements to be combined. Determining the acceptability of individual elements is not the immediate concern of the advocates of mixture. They displace the problem of selection one step by allowing many things to contribute to the total composition. The Picturesque shifts attention away from individual elements to the relation between them. Elements that might be considered inadmissible in other situations are not eliminated straightaway even though they could be. Instead a range of contrast is tolerated and the discussion becomes one of arrangement rather than of elimination.

no ranking no presumed hierarchy

When Price identifies the three qualities of roughness, sudden variation, and irregularity as the forces, or "causes," that make a picturesque composition, he is only stating half the case. The Picturesque does not rely exclusively on these qualities, but on their mixture into a composition that lacks them. The recommendation of these specific qualities was a response to the dominance of compositions that were considered too smooth and even. Because roughness, sudden variation, and irregularity are such salient sensory stimuli, they overshadowed the much more challenging principle of mixture.

not a formula

Price himself was misunderstood by those who focused exclusively on the three visual qualities. When he replied to landscape gardener Humphrey Repton's letter of July 1, 1794, he protested:

"From speaking warmly of certain wild, unpolished scenes, I have been represented as a person who, had I the power, would destroy all the comforts of a place; all gravel walks and shrubberies (in which case it would at least be proper to begin with my own), would allow no mowing, but wet everybody in high grass—tear their clothes with brambles and briars—send them up to their knees through dirty lands between two cart-ruts." Any implication that Price was simply advocating the replacement of one extreme by another was a direct challenge to the more fundamental principle of mixture. Price may have tried to anticipate such misrepresentation by identifying roughness and sudden variation as "opposite qualities." Continuous roughness is no better than continuous smoothness. Abrupt variation is the quality that ensures mixture.

William Mason's poem *The English Garden*, begun in 1767, with a new edition in 1783, seems to recommend mixture very directly. William, one of two gentlemen with this surname who contributed to the controversy surrounding garden design, the other being George, began as a liberal in political matters judging by his participation in the York Association for Parliamentary Reform, but, as things in France fell apart in the revolution and its aftermath, according to his estimation, he became firmly aligned with the British monarchy. In answer to the question whether one should "cut down ancient Vistas," he proposed that, rather than cutting down all traces of regularity framing the view, one should intersperse other trees with some of the oaks remaining in line. Tolerance for including patterns that subsequent taste rejects is the distinctive position that aligns Mason with the more complex Picturesque being presented here. But it is a position that Mason holds irregularly, even as his political allegiance shifted. Immediately preceding this expression of tolerance he recommends that whatever is straight should be melted into "fluent curves." In a note in Book 1, Mason quotes the seventeenth-century architect Henry Wooten to the effect that buildings and gardens are different things; "as fabricks should be regular, so gardens should be irregular, or at least cast into a very wild irregularity." While the idea of mixture is not new, the scale of its application is. The Picturesque applies it at both a much smaller and a much larger scale than did previous description.

Mixture was recognized as the source of the greatest aesthetic satisfaction by the philosopher Lord Kames in his *Elements of Criticism*. Both differences in similars and similarities in differences combine to produce surprise. Kames goes on to note that contrasts and alternations of similarity and difference cannot produce delightful surprise if they are repeated, however. The intermixture of grandeur with neatness, regularity with wildness, and gaiety with melancholy in visual as well as musical compositions makes them successful. The clearest use of contrast to produce a satisfying mixture occurs in Kames's description of garden art. "A garden near a great city ought to have an air of solitude," while an isolated garden should "avoid imitating nature, by taking on an extraordinary appearance of regularity and art." The contrast of the operations of the "busy hand of man" with the "waste country" will produce a "fine effect." Here is a clear example of the scale of mixture taking in a whole region.

Abrupt variation produces mixture through novelty. Richard Payne Knight recognized the salutary effect of "irritation" as an interruption of sensations that had become "stale and vapid" through repetition. "We naturally seek for some new impression that may restore that pleasure which we originally felt." But no sooner has he recommended novelty than he counters with the warning that this desire for change itself becomes morbid and vitiated if indulged to excess. This characteristic of recommending an absent or underrepresented stimulus separates the Picturesque from any argument appealing to an original starting point. The mixture is not directed to recovering a proper balance, but to maintaining a continuous sequence of contrast. What was once novel becomes stale and vice versa. The function of a compositional element is determined by its position in a sequence, not by its intrinsic nature.

Beyond surprise and refreshment, novelty provided a stimulus for curiosity. The variety introduced by novelty kept the composition from falling into uninteresting familiarity, at least for a time. One consequence of the resulting sensory agitation was to prevent attention from dwelling too long on any one aesthetic stimulus. For Price "irritation" was the source of active and lively pleasures. Soft and mild emotions were interrupted by emotions that were "eager, hurrying, impetuous." Prolonged contemplation of the finished beauty of art was displaced by a mobile, changeful, attention-seeking vividness and sharp impact. The pace of aesthetic perception was quickening.

The desire to mix contrasting sensory stimuli had become familiar in landscape compositions. The poet William Shenstone, whose Leasowes landscape garden was considered a major example of the new aesthetic mode in its mid-century emblematic phase, observed in his "Unconnected Thoughts on Gardening" (1765) that a series of lawns, "though ever so beautiful, may satiate and cloy, unless the eye passes to them from wilder scenes; and then they acquire the grace of novelty."

Breaking the continuity of an expected sequence bestows on the interruption a kind of originality. The abrupt change focuses attention on a stimulus that looks like a new beginning. When the abrupt change loosens tight strictures, it appears to be a return to an early stage in the sequence of increasing refinement; roughness is conventionally thought to precede finish: except in the Picturesque, when it follows it.

The Picturesque is clearly a response to a condition of plenitude. The notion that the sensory receptors lose their acuity when they are overstimulated suggests that too much of something brings on an overfull condition needing relief or change. The scale of the sensory vessel that is filled up is, apparently, rather small. Satiety is easily achieved. This smaller size of the vessel of experience, also known as the individual observer, is in step with an increase in the rate of sensory stimulation. Novelty is quickly apprehended and quickly passed beyond. Variety becomes a positive virtue. But, as Shenstone warns, if the variety is itself repeated in some kind of regular or expected pattern, it becomes uniformity at a larger scale. "A sufficient quantity of undecorated space is necessary to exhibit ... decorations to advantage." The scale at which this condition of plenitude operates is a crucial element in this discussion. For now, it is taken at the scale of the sensory receptors, but it reappears at the larger scale of the observer's relation to nature and to other people.

The shift in scale from the element itself to the pattern of successive elements is one of the ways picturesque compositions deal with the serious problem of connection. Shenstone addresses the matter of scale directly when he notes: "could we comprehend the universe, we might perhaps find it uniformly regular; yet the portions that we see of it habituate our fancy to the contrary." His recognition of the changing relations between part and whole reinforces the status of the Picturesque as a new way of framing perception. Deciding the characteristics of what one imagines to be a larger system based on a restricted sample makes the description of a composition very problematical.

The slow funding of an aesthetic experience was giving way to the sharp, penetrating impact of novelty or difference. Addison found in literary forms a comparable mixture in "the noble metaphor, [that] when it is placed to Advantage, casts a kind of Glory round it, and darts a Lustre through a whole sentence." A lustrous dart injects a point of light into a less brilliant surrounding at a scale significantly smaller than Longinus's sublime "flashing forth a thunderbolt." The light is quick and sharp. Its irritation interrupts a pattern of even sensory stimulation and the mind, or eye, immediately attends to the abrupt contrast. The abruptness of the unexpected produces novelty.

The discontinuity or abruptness produced by novelty can also frustrate or confuse conventional expectations. In his September 6, 1712, essay, Addison described "A Confusion of Kitchen and Parterre, Orchard and Flower Garden which lie so mixt and interwoven with one another, that if a Foreigner, who had seen nothing of our country, should be conveyed into my Garden at his first landing, he would look upon it as a natural Wildness, and one of the uncultivated Parts of our Country." It would "compose a Picture of the greatest Variety." In addition to laying out the heart of the picturesque principle of mixture, this description includes the freshness of a perceiving mind that arrives as a visitor.

The tourist is in search of novelty; he is not looking at things he already knows well, things that confirm his familiar conventions. The "Foreigner" cultivates perpetual surprise and pursues the curious. He moves about seeking delightful agitation. The mixture of many arrangements of the natural world in one place suggests confusion to those who are not on a holiday but are struggling through everyday survival based on clear categories. The mixture is itself a sign of "natural Wildness." The deception depends on the visitor imagining that what he sees, in part because he sees it for the first time, is an original condition. Wary travelers may discern the staged quality of the scene, or at least know that such a possibility exists. Whether the native populace would be fooled is very doubtful. They would recognize that the mixture is the result of a constructed composition. The result may indeed be confusing by those standards, but it would not be mistaken for natural wilderness.

Price elevates novelty's effects of variety and intricacy into a "universal source of pleasure." But he saves himself from the dogmatic assertion that his pleasure in roughness is universal. His contact with people whose experiences differ from his own forces him into a more general proposition. People who live among picturesque scenes appreciate ones with a directly opposite character, to Price's evident dismay. On a walk in Wales through "romantic" places with several natural cascades, he expressed his delight to the proprietor. "He was quite uneasy at the pleasure I felt, and seemed afraid I should waste my admiration. 'Don't stop at these things,' said he, 'I will shew you by and by one worth seeing.' At last we came to a part where the brook was conducted down three long steps of hewn stone: 'There,' said he, with great triumph, 'that was made by Edwards, who built Pont y pridd, and it is reckoned as neat a piece of mason-work as any in the country.' " This incident reveals the distance between someone whose limited resources lead him to value things neatly and firmly resistant, things that give evidence of some degree of mastery over nature, compared with someone whose ample resources and tourist's orientation allow a taste for looser and rougher things that can be enjoyed with no risk to himself.

[margin note: class issues / taste issue]

The battle to undermine the hegemony of the tight, strict geometry of French and Dutch garden designs by looser and more "natural" patterns had been largely won by the end of the eighteenth century. For Price and Knight the present enemy of mixture was Lancelot Brown. His phenomenal success in "improving" the great estates of England had produced a repetitive system of landscape composition. His departure from geometry had not produced variation, but sameness, not only in each individual garden, but in all his gardens taken together. Price's description of one of Brown's favorite features, the clump, tells how far he considered it to be from picturesque mixture. The Brownian clump of trees consisted of the "same tree, same age, all in a circle, as opposed to different trees, sizes, mixture of timber with thorns, hollies, full of variety, full of openings and hollows, trees advancing and retiring, changing at each step, new combinations, new lights and shades. But clumps, like compact bodies of soldiers, resist attack from all quarters: examine them in every point of view; walk around them; no opening, no vacancy, no stragglers! but in the true military character, ils font face partout." The military references reinforce that the enemy of mixture is system. Price remembers hearing that "when Mr. Brown was high-sheriff, some facetious person observing his attendant straggling, called out to him, 'Clump your javelin

men.' " Brown's landscape techniques became a "mechanical common-place operation." Walking around one of his clumps produced
"perpetual change without variety" and a defensive preservation of
identity.

Not only within the specifics of landscape gardening is mixture an issue. Crossing over the boundaries within any system of
categories excites some and horrifies others. For the latter, if distinctions are not cultivated, then things start to lose their identity
and measured consideration of them is impossible. The easy crossover between painting, landscape, poetry, and politics that one
encounters when reading about the Picturesque in the late eighteenth and early nineteenth centuries may be offensive, but the
arguments themselves depend on some degree of mixture. Comparisons made between literature and gardens carry features of one
realm over into another. This connection was explicit from the
beginnings of the discussion. Addison lines up kinds of poetry:
epigrams, romance, heroic, Pindaric; with kinds of gardening: par-
terres, grottoes, the gardens of Wise and LeNôtre. The overlap of
grottoes and romance is the easy, playful realm that became the
controversial site of the Picturesque.

The proposition that landscape design can gain from studying
painting, which was one of the major points of contention regarding the Picturesque, depends on the assumption that compositions
both sensory and intellectual can be based on a set of principles
that apply across various boundaries. Gardens, painting, literature,
and music are interchanged freely as arguments for the Picturesque
proceed. When Price is trying to establish the necessity for a
mixture of contrast within duration, he draws examples from
painting and music. "The mind . . . requires to be stimulated as well
as soothed, and there is in this, as in so many other instances, a
strong analogy between painting and music." Broad effects of light
and shadow affect the eye as mere harmony of sounds affect the ear;
"both produce a pleasing repose, a calm sober delight, which, if not

relieved by something less uniform, soon sinks into distaste and weariness."

Music and landscape design are drawn together when Price cites music's development as a model for landscape's. "Fugues and imitations in music began to grow out of fashion, about the time that terraces and avenues were demolished . . . Some of the greatest masters of music in later times, among whom Handel claims the highest place, have done what improvers might well have done; they have not abandoned symmetry, but have mixed it, (particularly in accompaniments,) with what is more wild and irregular." A passage from Handel's oratorio "Jephtha" is described to illustrate the point. Landscape can learn from musical compositions how "the ear, like the eye, tires of a repetition of the same flowing strain; it requires some marks of invention, of original and striking character as well as of sweetness in the melodies of a composer."

The licentious mixture of proper categories discomfits all who prefer tightly defined boundaries. George Mason, who as a director of the Sun Fire Office Insurance Company must have had a taste for accurate delineation of events and responsibilities, authored the *Essay on Design in Modern Gardening* (1768). He worried that writers on gardening were displaying dangerous foolishness by losing "themselves in the dream waste of metaphysical extravagancy." It was not so much that wandering was in itself misguided, only that it must be kept loose and suggestive. "There might be strong analogies between the pleasures of imagination and the mental affections and to trace them may be no unworthy employment of a liberal understanding." The transgression appeared when one tried to "systematically deduce every particle of the one from some correspondent part of the other." Composed wandering was an idea that simply crossed too many distinctions.

The second edition of Mason's *Essay*, published in 1795, greatly expanded his case and an appendix three years later added to the crescendo of the picturesque controversy by directly answering Price's essay of 1794. Price freely used Mason's poem because it "is so well known to all who have any taste for the subject, or for poetry in general, that it is hardly necessary to say, that the words between the inverted commas are chiefly taken from it." His admiration was not, however, without qualification. Mason's political alignment with Horace Walpole, the direct descendant of the court Whigs who had become inured to political power during the eighteenth century, indicated a deep conservatism that Price, the liberal Whig, could not abide.

Mason, like Price, was an eldest son, and his inheritance of lands and estates and his entry into the bar at the Inner Temple allowed him to mix in the world of gentlemen. His father acquired the estate of Porters to legitimize, in the traditional English way, a social stature that desperately needed it: he had made his money as a distiller. As someone who was establishing his legitimacy in rising social conditions, Mason was careful to espouse conservative tastes even as his elevation depended on a modern world that increasingly dismantled social boundaries.

Price also lived the life of a landed gentleman in the west county of Herefordshire as the eldest son who came into his fortune when he was fourteen. While at Eton he became friends with the liberal Whig Charles James Fox, joined in a play at Fox's family's home Holland House in 1761, and traveled with him in 1767 to Italy, Switzerland, and France. Richard Payne Knight also took his inheritance at an early age, traveled in Europe, built his west country estate, Downton Castle, and served with Price in Parliament as a partisan of Fox. His 10,000-acre estate included the iron works begun by his grandfather, but his alterations and additions, rather than continuing the exploitation of natural resources, used the accumulated monetary resources to contrive a desired appearance for aesthetic appreciation. Herefordshire was itself an example of mixture as its land was distributed between small owners, minor gentry, agriculture, and industry.

Knight's country estate on the border between Herefordshire

and Shropshire is as clear an example of mixture as one could ask. Begun while he was touring in Italy 1773-78, it may be the first example of a country seat intentionally irregular in plan and outline. Previously, architectural irregularities had arisen from successive additions. For some of Knight's contemporaries Downton Castle was a failed attempt at imitating Gothic. That charge is met directly when one sets foot in the principal rooms, which are anything but medieval or rustic. Classical orders and geometric room shapes suggest a complex intention for the whole that cannot be grasped by isolating the various parts. Knight described it thirty years after he built it—while acknowledging that now he might be able to do a better job—as a "house ornamented with what are called Gothic towers and battlements without, and with Grecian ceilings, columns and entablatures within." The result of his experiment is "a picturesque object, and an elegant and convenient dwelling." He extended his mixture by constructing a "Roman bath" whose three interconnecting chambers included a beehive dome, Gothic windows, brick walls and stone spar linings. As we picture Knight "wandering thro' romantic woods, planning and executing Improvements every morning," we must not forget that, when he was in London, Knight lived in Soho Square in a perfectly respectable urban house. Roughness and irregularity were fine for the country, but decorum and the conventions of urban life required classical forms in the city.

Price, too, felt that picturesque irregularity did not belong in town. In the midst of large settlements, the wealth, emulation, and comparisons necessary to the growth of the fine arts can flourish, but in the country, the architect is not so implicated by the accumulation of culture. A house in the country must respond to its setting. The adjustments to the specific location produce peculiarities and divergences from conventional rules of composition. The landscape and the building "suit and embellish each other." The argument that appropriateness is based on context reinforces that the Picturesque is about relationships between things.

The political correspondences with the Picturesque will receive more discussion later, but the specific principle of mixture can be cited in both a more recent estimation by Turberville that "Whiggism in its essence was typically English in its illogical combination of contraries, of radicalism with conservatism," and in a statement by Charles James Fox, leader of the liberal wing of the Whig Parliamentarians. Fox declared that he was "equally the enemy of all absolute forms of government, whether an absolute monarchy, an absolute aristocracy, or an absolute democracy. He was averse to all extremes, and a friend only to a mixed government." Such parallels between picturesque and political compositions are not only striking, they reveal a deep sympathy for a particular arrangement of parts into something like a whole.

When Uvedale Price and Richard Payne Knight engaged in their published exchanges over the Picturesque immediately before and after 1800, it was not easy to say if they were writing for gentlemen who were about to create picturesque compositions on their own estates or for those same gentlemen, as well as lesser men, who might engage in aesthetic contemplation of their own gardens or the countryside in Wales, Derbyshire, or the Continent. This confusion fueled much of the controversy surrounding the Picturesque. Those who approached the texts as handbooks for making a picturesque garden found vague directions full of contradictions. Those who thought they were reading a philosophical or literary treatise found more elevated considerations hobbled by the specifics of landscape improvement. Of course, the apparent confusion rose naturally from the attempt to present an elusive and complex argument linking patterns of landscape with patterns of political organization through a common mode of composition.

A picturesque mixture draws from sources that lie around it. The need for a term that partakes of contrasting aesthetic categories was one of the reasons for identifying the Picturesque initially. Specifically, by separating the two categories in his treatise in 1756

On the Sublime and the Beautiful, Edmund Burke prompted the creation of a middle term to describe compositions that partook of both. Price, who generally favored Burke's analysis, clearly located the Picturesque "between beauty and sublimity." In that mediating position, the two contrasting categories were "blended, but perfectly distinct." The vacancy between the Beautiful and the Sublime was filled up by a term that "corrects the langour of beauty, or the horror of sublimity."

Sublimity relies on an enormity and vastness that seemed out of reach for landscape improvement. Its remoteness from human ingenuity shifted attention to the opposite category of beauty. The distinction between the Picturesque and the Beautiful generated considerable discussion. William Gilpin's popularization of the Picturesque in his various accounts of tours around England and his very accessible recommendations regarding sketching and painting moved Knight and Price to take up the more complex implications. For Gilpin beauty itself included some sharp "irritation" of the senses. For Price, beauty was all smooth and soft; it is soothing and utterly satisfying as on a warm, genial day. "We are unwilling to move, almost to think, and desire only to feel, to enjoy." Beauty is passive. That characterization, of course, led him to propose a corrective that was primarily sharp and abrupt. "How different is that active pursuit of pleasure, when the fibres are braced by a keen air, in a wild, romantic situation; when the activity of the body almost keeps pace with that of the mind, and eagerly scales every rocky promontory, explores every new recess. Such is the difference between the beautiful and the picturesque." Knight as well as Gilpin found Price's beauty too obviously a "straw man" set up for purposes of the desired conclusion.

As a middle term the limits and boundaries of the Picturesque are hard to prescribe. Rather than being an independent element, it may only be an admixture, a corrective. Because a corrective is effective only when it assumes sufficient similarity to attach itself to

its subject, so does the Picturesque when united to either the
Beautiful or the Sublime adjust to the circumstances. The independent identity of such an idea is always in jeopardy.

Price and Knight's controversy over the Picturesque developed, in part, from their different estimations of Burke's argument.
Price generally accepted it; Knight did not. George Mason and
Knight both remarked on Price's acceptance of Burke's categories.
Knight seized on what he considered a serious confusion in Burke's
and Price's analysis of beauty by pointing out that their definition of
"smooth and undulating surfaces, flowing lines and colors," mis-
places beauty in the things of sight habitually associated with
beauty rather than in the "intellectual qualities of things." The
Scottish philosopher Dugald Stewart observed that "Price invented
the Picturesque to correct Burke because he believed Burke and did
not correct or critique, but accepted his definition of Beauty." Price
accepted Burke's categories and dealt with difficulties he found in
the argument, not by restructuring it, but by adding a new term in
between the two given by Burke. This alteration by addition created a more complex mixture, rather than the clarification produced
by revolution. Stewart, follower and friend of the associationists
Thomas Reid and Archibald Alison, had placed the operation of
mental processes very near the center in his analysis of matters of
taste.

The absence of explicit structure in the mental processes that
followed on raw retinal stimuli led Burke and Price to posit fixed
standards for aesthetic matters based on the constant status of
physical objects or our sensory apparatus. The lack of connective
mental structure was compensated by the fixity of the two parts
that constituted sensory experience, that is, sight and the objects of
sight. They were irreducible elements, not subject to varying interpretations. Knight, along with the associationist Alison, required
some structure in the mental processes to account for the variability
exhibited by different people and different cultures in their aesthet-

ic preferences. For him structure was directed to preserving mixture, not leveling it, which is what Price accused him of doing.

When Price addressed the matter of associationism directly,
he acknowledged that perception combines impressions on the
senses with reflections in the mind. By recognizing that associations, particularly with reference to "utility," affect one's response to
a landscape scene, he emphasized associationism's applicability to
the lower aspects of human experience.

In spite of his sympathy with Burke's aesthetic analysis, Price
explicitly rejects George Mason's characterization of Burke's "doctrine and system." For Knight, Burke and Price placed too much
emphasis on the role of "sensual impressions" which seemed to
result in a completely unstructured aesthetic experience wholly
unsuited for aesthetic speculation. Such immediate and perishing
material tended toward a radical empiricism that could not explain
connections between sensory stimuli. Knight required some means
to connect aesthetic responses and, at the same time, to take account of memory, imagination, and the passions. Such structures
could not be suppressed totally in the interest of avoiding the
tyranny of systematic organization.

The arguments between Price and Knight appeared trivial to
some observers at the time, but we can see that, with a common
interest in preserving mixture, they came up with two methods for
doing so. Each saw in the other's method the potential compromise
with system. In determining the balance between persisting structure and immediate sensory stimulation, Knight included more
structure, Price more perishing stimuli. Price and Knight diverged
on the very point of balance between tyranny and license: Knight
feared tyranny less and license more, Price feared license less and
tyranny more.

In contrast to the mixture of nature and artifice recommended
by the Picturesque, nature itself was made to represent the original,
redemptive model by some writers on garden art. To them any

suggestion that mixture or confusion had a place in the composition of landscapes seemed manifestly unnatural. R. L. Gerardin, vicomte d'Ermenonville, offered a French contribution to this discussion that appeared originally in 1777 and was translated in 1783 by David Malthus, brother of the economist and population prognosticator. Malthus's introduction to the English edition of *An Essay on Landscape* supported the work of Gerardin because it aligned with William Mason's "very beautiful poem" and Horace Walpole's conservative comments on garden art. Malthus admired Gerardin's book for its desire to recapture an origin for man's relation to nature, a desire not surprising in a patron of Rousseau. By joining beauty with utility, he did not engage in a critique of either representation or the whimsical play with layers of meaning. Malthus cites classical fragments from Juvenal and Cicero, Theocritus and Virgil as links to contemporary discussions of a cultural canon whose authority paralleled that of nature. The classical precedents for delight in untamed nature were, of course, well known. Whether Horace in his Epistles longs for the woods or country life or Virgil's Eclogues or Georgics recommend the simple life, English gentlemen had such images at their disposal.

By quoting Dryden's "Satires" of Juvenal, Malthus's introduction places "marble caves" against "first-created green" graced by an "urn of native stone." If original green is clearly nature's product, then any object fashioned by man's hand opposed it, except, of course, if it were made of native stone. The material given by nature is the key to naturalness even if human action separates it from its proper place. Even though a cave suggests nature, if it is made of marble, it is an intrusion (except as it is native to the place, one imagines). Cicero, as well, is called upon to establish the terms of natural virtue. In his Second Dialogue on Laws, Atticus rhetorically questions Cicero: "Who is there, Marcus, that looking at these natural falls, and these two rivers, which form so fine a contrast, would not learn to despise our pompous follies, and laugh at artificial Niles, and seas in marble; for as in our late argument you referred all to nature, so, more especially in things which relate to the imagination, is she our sovereign mistress." The classical models of imagination are grounded in the world in which they were composed. The Romans lived in a landscape that had "so many stations (to use a term of our present tourists) in that universal garden which formed the shore of the Mediterranean." The poets looked around them and composed their verses from what they saw.

The Greeks and Romans, being closer to the original condition of nature, and presumably less capable of altering it, could only choose and admire natural scenes. Knowing classical landscapes primarily through poetry emphasizes the imagination rather than tools for digging. "Let it be the glory of the modern gardening to imitate, to compose, or even to create." The eighteenth-century Englishman imagines that he is not so passive as his ancient mentors. (However, choosing and admiring were activities engaged in by the tourists moving about on the newly improved highways in England.) The modern gardener, inspired by classical models, intervenes more directly. The three levels of intervention set out by the introduction: imitation, compositon, and creation, ascend to the highest point of origination even as they depart from origin.

The traditional classical education prepared the English gentleman to make connections between the poetical descriptions and familiar scenes around England. A passage from Cicero becomes "the most perfect of English gardens." Matlock in Derbyshire "resembles this celebrated vale of antiquity [the Thessalian Temple] in many striking particulars."

Nature and the conventions of classical culture each served as foundations for stable, authoritative, aesthetic constructions. The appeal to such sanctioned sources may be argued in terms that seem to set up a contradiction between nature and convention, but neither is willing to replace its claims of absolute reliability by a recognition of its self-referential construction. Mixture itself can be proposed as a stable, optimal condition only by seeing its prevention of homogenization as a constant that lies behind obvious changes. Such a continuous reframing of the phenomenon as whole becomes a part serves to overcome the inertia of certainty.

When writing *The Progress of a Civil Society* (1796), two years after his poem *The Landscape*, Knight continued his adherence to the ideal of mixture in his praise of Lucretius's style. For Knight, the Roman Epicurean's Latin avoided gigantic exertion that strained after "supernatural sublimity" even as it refrained from "affected ease and colloquial vulgarity." Since exertion is evident at a glance and affected ease and vulgarity can be discovered soon enough, Knight advocates picturesque uncertainty, or mystery as it is also called, by citing poetry that does not expend all its resources in a massive effort and, at the same time, does not underplay its capacities so egregiously as to call attention to the disparity between effort and resources. Affected ease is not *sprezzatura*, and colloquial vulgarity is not nonchalance.

Improvement of the land, whether for agricultural or scenic purposes, could be carried out according to a similar ideal loosely correlating effort and resources. One of the greatest of them, the earl of Leicester, realized the gap that could appear between intention and result. When complimented on the completion of his great design at Holkham, he replied: "It is a melancholy thing to stand alone in one's country; look round; not a house is to be seen but mine; I am the Giant of Giant-castle, and have eat [sic] up all my neighbors." This incident is mentioned in a note in Robert Potter's *Observations of the Poor Laws* (1775) after referring to Oliver Goldsmith's "Deserted Village," which clearly represented a villager's viewpoint in an estate similar to Holkham. The suppression of mixture or differences seems like a reasonable course, if one is making one's own composition. However, when exclusion is total, an emptiness appears. Not to exercise all one's resources in the process of perfecting the composition seems a strange thing to do at the outset, but once total success has been achieved, the desire to have withheld some effort arises as a kind of nostalgia for a mixture suppressed.

Mixture is opposed to system. Knight and Price both attack the devastating effect of system on a civil society as well as on its garden art. For Knight, sophistry is a model of tyrannical system. Its only characteristic feature is its frigidity. Abstract reason, cold and mechanical, suffers no deviations or alternatives. It is selfish, isolated, confined. It "cramps vigor, . . cools fervor," and "kills Fancy and Fiction." The antidote to its influence is the Muses' song. Life and art unite in their opposition to death and rigid rule. Fancy and fiction are not excluded, the desire to believe is not coldly repressed, it is allowed to act warmly and fully, but it is not permitted to go too long unchecked, either by doubt or a contrasting desire. It is not too far off, however, to imagine that "truth" can be approximated simply by entertaining a sufficient number of fictions.

Complexity is the sign of vigor. "Complicated laws arise from complicated interests, and produce republics better balanced, than if they had been planned by prospective wisdom." The prejudice Knight is supporting justifies the accumulation of civil structures and the incremental adjustments they make to changing circumstances. To imagine thinking through such a complex set of relationships at any given moment is sheer folly. The only conceivable result of such arrogance is a tyrannical abstraction that can only level necessary differences and dilute a vigorous mixture. In what might pass for support for a democratic structure, Price finds a rich mixture on a national scale "if each improved his own place, according to general conceptions drawn from nature and pictures there might in time be a great variety in the styles of improvement."

When Edmund Burke could no longer tolerate the violent leveling forces of the French Revolution, he attacked abstract political ideals precisely for their systematic destruction of accumulated social and political mixture. His attack separated him from his longtime friend and parliamentary colleague, Charles James Fox, who supported the French Revolution long after more timid Englishmen had run for defensive cover. The sharp difference between the two Whig politicians may be ascribed to their support of mixture at different scales: Fox at a broader, more confident scale; Burke, the newcomer to the circle of Whig grandees, at a smaller, more apprehensive scale. Burke's appeals to the singular significance of real events accumulating without apparent plan would seem to parallel the picturesque ideal of composition. The historical events that had brought England to its present constitution could only be compromised by an abstraction that claimed to underlie them and any such claim was only a pernicious attempt to substitute unreliable machinations of the mind for solid reality. Fox's confidence could easily shade off into systematic unresponsiveness, while Burke's could perpetually destroy any continuity except as exercised through circumstantial force. A contrary difference surfaces when one recognizes that Fox was a great companion on the personal level, while Burke was willing to sacrifice such smaller-scale connection to abstract principle.

Mixture depends on things already being present to mix. In landscape design, it means combining two givens: nature and human artifice. The characteristic picturesque scene includes traces, at least, of obviously formal arrangements blended with and in contrast to the irregularities appearing through the progression of nature and time. Because the Picturesque starts, so to speak, one step up the ladder from propositions about the origins of either nature or humanity, it avoids entanglement in an endless regression pursuing a genuine starting point. As a result the Picturesque does not define itself through internal evidence in the ultimately vain attempt to produce a resistant identity. By beginning its operation after the elements with which it works have gotten their start, it freely combines and arranges. Such freedom draws the charge of promiscuity from anyone who clings to assertions that must begin in some unique claim to originality.

These comments are not solely interpretations gained by looking back through two hundred years of speculation. Uvedale Price himself suffered the misunderstanding that almost inevitably follows an argument for mixture. Humphrey Repton, like Lancelot

Brown, directed digging and flooding and planting in accordance with his own ideas of garden art. For him speculation was unnecessary and probably misleading. His letter to Price after the first publication of Price's essay *On the Picturesque* derided any extended consideration of painting or philosophical musings and gladly sought to catch Price in the contradictions that arose from trying to mix artifice and nature. Price responded: "Whoever reads your letter without having read my book, just probably concludes that I am a sort of tiger, who pass my life in a jungle, with no more idea of the softer beauties of nature than that animal. I fear that I am not less exposed to an imputation of a very different kind; and that I should not be surprised were some wrong-headed friend of Mr. Gilpin to represent me as a man so in love with smoothness, as to have no relish for what is rough, abrupt and picturesque. . . . He might treat me as a false friend, and ask whether a man can be a true lover of the picturesque, who allows, that near the house it ought to be sacrificed to neatness and convenience." The reversals in the evaluation of forms when they are either predominant or when they are mixed in to break dominance undermine any absolute reading. As the circumstances surrounding a composition change, the parts that constitute it are reevaluated. As a consequence it is easy to make the whole process seem like the height of folly, shifting fitfully about in search of its true goal. The observation that "it may very nearly be said that equality is deformity" only seems to prove how ludicrous the whole notion of the Picturesque really is.

If Price is the proponent of a Picturesque misunderstood to be nothing more than roughness, irregularity, and abrupt variation, then any mixture of these qualities with their opposites is clear evidence of flimsy conviction. It is fair to say that Repton's misrepresentation is not all that far away from what Price had actually advocated in his initial statements. It is not difficult to understand Repton's confusion when, after reading how Price values roughness, irritation, and novelty, he proceeds to describe the ground immediately around a house as follows: "To go at once from art [building] to simple, unadorned nature, is too sudden a transition, and wants that sort of gradation and congruity, which except in particular cases, is so necessary in all that is to please the eye and the mind." Repton's letter happily provided the opportunity for Price to clarify that roughness, irregularity, and abrupt variation were important, not so much in and for themselves, as for their contribution to mixture. By dwelling upon those less observed, less obvious and generally less attractive beauties, some had asserted that he, "not only preferred such scenes as were merely rude and picturesque, but excluded all others."

In an attempt to clarify further any misunderstanding, Price said in summary that "the whole purpose" of his work came down to mixing the qualities of smoothness, distinctness, formality, and the like, with the "striking effects . . . of a totally opposite nature," not abandoning or neglecting them. "Such a mixture so sanctioned, appears to have such obvious and superior claims over any narrow system of exclusion, that it is hard to conceive how a system of that kind could long prevail among men of liberal and highly cultivated mind."

The appeal to men of liberal and highly cultivated mind reinforces the connection of this discussion of landscape design with the even broader issue of how assertions should be made and control exercised.

> I should be very sorry to be suspected of having combated the despotism of others, in order to establish any arbitrary opinions of my own: but a physician must proportion his remedy to the degree, as well as to the nature of the disease; and bareness, monotony, and want of connection, are in a high degree the diseases of modern improvement. Had the opposite system prevailed, (and in the revolutions to which fashion is subject, it may prevail) had all buildings of every kind been encumbered by trees, or had they, from a rage for the picturesque, been fantasically designed,

with an endless diversity of different heights and breaks, with odd projections and separations—I should equally have taken my arguments from the works of eminent painters as well as of architects, against such a departure from all grandeur, elegance, and simplicity. The best preservative against flatness and monotony on the one hand, and whimsical variety on the other, is an attentive study of what constitutes, the grand, the beautiful, and the picturesque in buildings, as in all other objects.

Price's plea demonstrates the correlation between compositions of visual stimuli and of social relations. His recommendations regarding landscape design are immediately read as recommendations regarding how people should live. His point is misunderstood because of the tangle of interrelations that link one realm directly to another. One is not primary and therefore illustrated by the other. The compositional argument applies to both.

In the clearest possible terms, Price positions his work to refer to the relationship between parts, rather than to the parts for themselves. It may come as a surprise to realize that the Picturesque is not about the inherent virtues of roughness, irregularity, and abrupt variation, but about their contribution to a larger composition. Its motivation is to keep things alive by mixing in the marginal qualities, to maintain vividness, to resist the tendency for systematic application of any form of selection to become despotic.

PASTORAL

The pastoral mode in poetry, originating in Hellenistic Alexandria with Theocritus and brought to the height of art by Virgil two and a half centuries later in Augustan Rome, is a literary form artfully mixing rusticity and sophistication. A rural setting as well as vernacular language and subjects contribute to the mix. The appearance of rusticity belies the self-consciousness employed to fashion the picture. Real shepherds may play the pipes and sing about love, but they do so directly, not as a reflective representation of nature and art. Only someone who no longer, if ever, relied on the earth for direct sustenance can manage the distancing required to make art out of the pastoral setting.

The appearance of the pastoral mode signals another step away from an imagined authenticity toward perpetual artifice. When Theocritus, around 270 B.C., set his shepherds in the pastures of Cos or Sicily, he supplied them with a consciousness and literacy they had not acquired through communion with sheep. These swains "lived below their intellectual means." The informality, weakness, and humility of the pastoral setting and the figures sketched in it are used to displace the absent, or "higher," power that ultimately sustains the whole poetic image.

The evolution of rural song into a literary category is scarcely a surprising process. Consciousness, frightened by its distance from a memory of naturalness, casts about for renewal in the melodies of those who appear to remain imbedded in a natural continuity. Theocritus, born in Sicily, knew more about pastoral life than if he had always lived around the court and library in Alexandria, where he composed much of his poetry. The appearance of the pastoral form in cosmopolitan Alexandria of the first Ptolemies is the literary embodiment of a crisis in the direct expression of power. Not only did Ptolemy II pursue a delicate balancing act between energetic Hellenism and ancient Egyptian tradition, but the polyglot cultural makeup of the great city, "by" but not "of" Egypt, blurred the direct expression of any one tradition by merging it with other tributary streams. Indirection and complexity had replaced the singular power of the fifth-century polis and its political art.

Theocritus supported Callimachus's argument for a briefer, more accessible form for poetry than the epic. The grandeur of the epic seemed inaccessible. Poetry, as Edgar Allan Poe would assert two thousand years later, was the brief assault on prosaic consciousness, not a prolonged seige. Along with Theocritus's use of dialect, this preference for shorter forms seems less a strategic posture than an attempt to retain continuity with an earlier literary condition. But these choices clearly indicate a desire to pull back from the full exercise of rationalized literary power. The idylls are acknowledged "little pictures."

Pastoral was given a lowly rank in the literary hierarchy. Its opposite number was epic. To spend time on pastoral poetry was evidence of an adolescent level of skill or capacity. To edit down the epic sweep by suggesting that the pastoral warranted serious attention upset proper relations of importance. (The status of landscape painting in the eighteenth century was argued on similar grounds.) To write in a vein that deliberately included awkwardnesses presented a disturbing irresolution that drew attention to the relations between writer, poem, and reader. The gap that appears when an artificer takes up a task that does not appear to engage all of his prowess leaves room for self-conscious reflection on the process by both the author and the reader.

There is little metaphor in Theocritus. Images and the things they resemble are kept separate; natural objects retain their identity. The literary device of inventory maintains this independence and precludes a hierarchical priority. This is not to say, however, that the natural objects float randomly. There is, as in any rural tradition, a general and vaguely felt kinship of all the parts of the world that does not need to be made explicit. To the poet and reader, a list seems "natural," untainted by intellectual systems of order. The simplicity of "just the facts" restores to a sophisticated mind an openness, an opportunity to look at the raw material as if for the first time, setting aside previous structures and pretending to be back at the dawn of consciousness, a state of literary "under-development." It is part of the myth of freedom searching for origin. The audience reading Theocritus would know both the literary controversy arguing for simplicity in a metropolitan world increasingly separated from rural roots and the possibility that the pastoral arose out of a tradition of poetical lament to become a moment of contemplation in a shady spot, often near a pool, where songs of unrequited love are sung.

The idealism of the pastoral not only creates a peaceful contentment, but it comments on striving complexity. Its deliberate naïveté is not simple. The goatherd responds to a friendly challenge to a singing match in Idyll 7: "I hate the builder who tries to raise / his roof as high as Oromedon's peak / no less than I hate those cocks who strut / in the Muse's yard, wretchedly trying / to match Chio's nightingale with their crows." Obvious grandeur is forever the antithesis and yet pride for winning a song contest held in the shade of an osier tree is acceptable. Striving has some limits that can fit comfortably into a pastoral poem.

The literary landscape of the pastoral was created from the perspective of urban traditions, whether third-century B.C. Theocritus or first-century B.C. Virgil. The virtues of a simpler life embodied in the shepherds were admired through the windows of the court or its outposts. Whether Roman aristocrats retired to their villas in the hills outside the city or in the provinces or the younger son of the Japanese emperor built a tea pavilion at Katsura in the seventeeth century to overlook the melon fields west of Kyoto, the location may seem rustic even as the conversation or individual musing is extremely sophisticated. The actors in the pastoral poems, if one imagined them as "real," were engaged in the langorous task of herding only because they did not in fact depend on it for their livelihood. Subsidies of money, time, and education were required to support the artifice. What bound all these contradictions into a whole was the art of song. The lyric moment, usually in the stillness of midday, substitutes the instant of spatial experience for the moving sequence of time. This focused frame of life does not anneal stresses in the white heat of power, but deflects contradictions into a pool of shade fashioned by art.

the pastoral as well as the picturesque are about deflection

Harsh poetical expression or vernacular language more characteristic of Theocritus, but also appearing occasionally as in Virgil's earliest eclogue, second in the collection, lines 25–26, may be "technical incompetence or deliberate artifice." One can dismiss the harsh elisions as youthful awkwardness or as deliberate roughness put in the mouth of the shepherd Corydon as he describes himself as not so ugly when he saw himself in the calm waters of the sea. Not being sure if we are in the presence of incompetence or artifice is the heart of the matter. The poetic artifact is not immediately met; its status is not immediately grasped. Before we can go forward, we must decide what it is. This uncertainty delays and complicates our response. Is the poet clumsy or is the rudeness part of the story? Is the harshness unconscious or an apparent lapse that can be risked because the poet is in complete control; is it weakness or power? This question relates the pastoral to the Picturesque and to certain political ideals as well.

If Theocritus's idylls are closer to a tradition of rural song, his first steps into rural artifice were followed up and refined by Virgil in his eclogues. With Virgil we encounter a much more explicit use of the pastoral for political as well as literary purposes. The First Eclogue sets the course of the literary genre. Its dialogue tells of two forms of displacement: one shepherd driven away from his accustomed place on the land by economic necessity and the other removed from the effects of that necessity by intervention from power residing in the city.

The migrant Meliboeus is being thrown out of his farm and from under his turf-clad roof by economic resources wielded by a returning soldier or assimilated barbarian. Tityrus sits aside from the road leading to exile, at ease in his familiar world, piping to the woodland muse, protected from the forces that are driving his friends away. He can maintain the stability of his pastoral world because he left it and went to the city to appeal for the creation of a sanctuary to which he could return. The prolongation of his world is physically continuous but is now a different thing, sustained by power that is not present in that world. He now inhabits art.

Tityrus draws a distinction between the nearby town to which he has been connected by daily economic ties and the capital city, Rome. The town did not support his desire for leisure: its practical response to his georgic efforts causes him to call it "thankless." He had to go to Rome to find sympathy for his age and his art. His consciousness now seems lost in the constructed harmony. He is somehow unsympathetic to his friend's plight, while Meliboeus's grief connects him with the practical details of the land and the reality of the human condition.

The slenderness and delicacy of the pastoral flourishes in leisure and relative abundance, as Tityrus suggests when he tells Meliboeus that he is welcome to stay the night and enjoy apples, chestnuts, and cheeses. But it is not only that. The contrast between the two shepherds sets up the tension that is generated when the sources of the pastoral composure are taken into account. Order and confinement are apparently produced by the idealism of the poet-singer who is not supposed to understand anything beyond simple pleasures. It is an art that takes account of complication not within itself, as part of its explicit attention, but by provoking it through its beautiful absence. The consciousness is not in the poem, but is displaced into the consciousness of the reader. The pastoral deals with conflict not by being tense but by being gracefully oblivious.

The clarity of this message, its distance from a Theocritan world of enumeration and naïveté are unmistakable. And the subsequent history of the poetical type in Western literature works and reworks the implications of Virgil's masterpieces. A picture of nature enjoyed when the life at court has become either hazardous or decadent is sketched by the Renaissance pastoralist Jacopo Sannazaro in the preamble, completed by 1489, to his *Arcadia*: "The lofty, densely foliaged trees with which simple nature, unaided by art, has covered the summit of the most fearful mountains are generally more pleasing to the viewer than are those carefully nurtured and skillfully developed plants destined to ornament gardens." He links political issues to sensory stimulation by asserting that "The ear is more enchanted by the warbling of birds flying in liberty in the woods than by the carefully studied song of birds enclosed in magnificent cages in the heart of towns." Pastoral poetry, picturesque landscape, and freedom are clearly associated in a more or less unselfconscious way. Tasso's *Jerusalem Delivered*, written in 1581 to rival Ariosto's *Orlando Furioso*, includes a stanza that reinforces the mixture lying at the heart of this attitude toward control: "You would judge (so mingled is negligence with care) both the grounds and their improvements only natural. It seems an act of nature, that for her own pleasure playfully imitates her imitator." The latter sentence more or less sums up the picturesque attitude with its uncertain appearance, playfulness, and layers of representation.

Virgil radically extended the narrow range of the pastoral in the Fourth Eclogue by suggesting that "otium" or composure can be victorious over time's displacement. The pastoral proposes only a momentary suspension of these processes. Through the power of song, of artifice, an eddy of stability is created in the midst of change. The impossibility of satisfying such a desire and yet the attempt to do so are other instances of the pastoral poem engaging the reader in a dialogue about its status. We go forward to suspend movement, carrying with us all the time the irritating knowledge that we are being swept along even as we dream. To propose an end to these internal stresses, as Virgil does in the Fourth Eclogue, is to undermine fatally the pastoral form. Victory and purgation are utterly antithetical to the poetical mode because the pain that gives artifice its meaning is wiped out by the end of time. The idea of time progressing to some permanent "salvation" that resolves conflict seriously compromises the pastoral ideal of freedom, which exists only on the margin. Such a resolution beyond the confines of art explicitly engages the larger world that is not present in the pastoral. And an exultant pastoral flies in the face of the pliant, humble character which is at its heart. When the meek inherit the earth, the pastoral is not, at last, triumphant; there is no pastoral at all.

freedom on the margin, a metaphor

it is not about ultimates

The English pastoral tradition coming out of the seventeenth and into the eighteenth century can be interpreted variously as an evolution of literary convention self-consciously continuing classical traditions or as a social instrument of deception draping economic power in a "natural" and informal costume. The effort to escape the confines of the pastoral tradition of the Augustans, whose artifice had become so artificial as to be unconvincing, led to an increasing realism. Epic heroes were clearly imaginary, while the English pastoral was to be more empirical. It added the vividness of reality itself, its immediate impact on the senses and its immediate comprehensibility. Early eighteenth-century observations on the pastoral and landscape painting lost sight of the contribution of artifice only because of the more obvious artifice of other, more highly placed genres. Suppressing the artifice in favor of nature set the pastoral on a Romantic course that lost the crucial tension between the two that makes the pastoral so cunning.

The closer relation between life and the land that supports it as depicted in the georgic form appears in the English pastoral as a tension between social observation and literary harmony. Ideals of justice and literal truth can be unselfconsciously part of the pastoral only by displacing its more insidious power to disturb any claims of the redemptive exercise of power. The georgic, as a parallel poetic form practiced by Virgil, makes a much more direct relation between man and nature than does the pastoral. The tradition of writing about the pursuit of metabolic survival and its enjoyment focuses on simple pleasures and pragmatic wisdom. It is more naturalistic in its presentation of the "facts" of rural life. As a consequence it can be called upon as a corrective to the pastoral when artifice becomes tyrannical. The eighteenth-century georgic appears as a bracing antidote to Augustan sophistication and serves as a way to comment on economic and social strains in the English countryside. The distance separating the georgic from the pastoral is produced by the realistic certainty of the former and the free play between artifice and nature of the latter.

The reintroduction of ambiguity, or at least an intensification of the tension between art and nature, occurred with changes in the way the land was owned, consumed, and perceived. Recently arrived landowners used poetry as a propaganda tool to make their place seem an ancient right. Consciousness of the changes affecting the land slipped into poems celebrating Penshurst or Appleton House, but the pastoral needed to go back to the country after having spent too much time looking at the world from the mirrors inside the villa. The pastoral impulse to retreat from courtly artifice and excess and to reassert the virtues of a simpler life close to nature gained strength in poems like Oliver Goldsmith's "Deserted Village" of 1769.

Goldsmith's poem will absorb our attention because it is the absent half of Virgil's First Eclogue. It is the story of the place Meliboeus left behind. "The Deserted Village" is built on the social and economic changes that underlie what at first seems like a familiar opposition between luxury and simplicity. But the poet of eighteenth-century England is not part of the scene; he is returning to it in hopes of finding the place he remembers from his youth preserved like Tityrus's farm. However, "Sweet Auburn," like Meliboeus's farm, has not been protected from change. Its children, too, are "far, far away." The newly arrived power in Auburn, like the victorious Roman soldier rewarded for his exploits or the non-Roman rewarded for his loyalty, is at a scale beyond the village. Luxuries fly to it from around the world. The local detail of person or place is lost on an owner who, by looking beyond Auburn or Meliboeus's farm, reduces it to an undifferentiated category. This loss of detail is accomplished by tyranny; its appearance is unvaried; its result is to produce deserts.

Because the new owner is only marginally concerned with the village, it has suffered neglect: clear streams are clogged, grass grows over the walls, and trees once trimmed for shade are shapeless ruins now. Compared with neat and clean productivity, this neglect is not picturesque. The ambiguity that exists between the pastoral and the reader as he tries to decide the status of the poem and its occasional awkwardness has become firmly imbedded in the poem itself. The poem is explicitly a return and a remembrance.

The opposition between "light labor" and "toiling pleasure," between graceful swains and "Unwieldy wealth" is standard pastoral fare. But the native son, who took all that the village had to offer and went on to acquire distant learning and who now returns with the expectation of being welcomed, vividly points up the ambiguity of the artifice imposed from without. He is returning with power and perception gained from the antithetical world of the city. He expects to slip back into the scene, not quite unnoticed, but with a gentle acknowledgment of his position. He admits the pride, but tries to keep it from making him too much larger than those who stayed behind, by virtuously insisting that he is still smaller than the "cumbrous Pomp" that has established itself since his departure. He wants to retire here, take his ease, live in the classical posture of "otium," supported not by his daily labor, but by the accumulated resources brought in from outside. These resources will be spent in such a way as to preserve his comfort without ostentation. He has become the tourist, the summer person. He dresses down toward the locals, but he does not own the town.

Goldsmith notices that the "improvements" effected in Auburn by the new landowner are not directed to keeping the land productive, but for visual delight. "The country blooms—a garden and a grave." The garden is still a garden, not a landscape whose natural appearance one can be sure about. The support for its creation is not derived locally. The grave is explicitly where the poet's memory of his happy youth is buried. The realization that every garden inters the memory of an unspoiled world lies outside the poet's consciousness. What Goldsmith has done in "The Deserted Village" is to move part of the ambiguity that lay between the reader and the pastoral poem into the poem itself, but he has not removed all of the complexity from that intermediate region. He still imagines that the poem is a lament for resolution.

The dominant power in Auburn imposes not only toil, but pleasures that are the products of "unfeeling" trade. Its mobility and lack of original place make trade an enemy of the still, humble pastoral image. But poetry, too, is set in motion by trade. The pastoral poet and his poem must bid Auburn farewell. Their self-image of independence, compromised by the presence of trade, of power located outside the image, can be preserved only by dislocating themselves once again. But to lament the parting is to miss the point. From Virgil's First Eclogue the genre recognizes that it is always dependent; its posture of independence always draws attention to the configuration of power underutilized. By blithely asserting its independence in the poem, the pastoral glances at the world outside itself and almost coyly invites questions about its status.

The pastoral genre, by using the rural world of shepherds, hills, and streams, makes the first impression of nature a question rather than an answer. What looks simple with its rustic setting and subjects, what looks weak and poor compared to military heroes, the power of the court, and vigorous economic activity is not simple. The poem is a representation whose artifice at once hides itself and envelops the reader. As the Elizabethan poet George Puttenham noted, rather than being direct either about its subject or its means, the pastoral manages, "under the veil of homely persons, and in rude speeches to insinuate and glance at larger matters." Of course these larger matters could be, and are, addressed directly in many other modes, but in the pastoral they are addressed along the margin.

The pastoral must answer the question: what is gained by not using the direct, powerfully focused approach? The sharpest attack on the pastoral is that its insinuation and glancing attention conceal all sorts of manipulation. By not being direct, the larger issues are not presented so that the reader can meet them for what they are and be moved by appeals that are clear. From this point of view, surreptitious maneuvering, lies, and misrepresentation can be hidden within a mode that sidles around "larger matters." Such an approach cannot be trusted. Rather than seeing this apparent lack of trustworthiness as a flaw, the pastoral makes the point that critical reading can never be allowed to slumber in some reassuring aura of trust. The direct approach, by using a mode that is associated with "just the facts" or some other convention of trustworthiness, is far more insidious than a mode that uses artifice to create a tension warning of potential difficulties. The pastoral explicitly mixes the ease of unthreatening rural scenes with a potentially unsettling set of questions about nature and art, liberty and artifice. And by locating part of the question, not in the poem itself, but in the space surrounding the poem and the reader, it challenges any easy reading.

The second attack on the pastoral is that it is an easy way to seem concerned with "larger matters." Larger matters are difficult; they have their own discipline and merely to glance at them only avoids the discipline required for dealing with important things. It is used by those who only want the credit of dealing with important things without earning the right to do so. If the pastoral set itself up

does this through language

as a replacement for the epic or other extended modes, such an attack might be justified. But precisely because the pastoral is a momentary posture, its flash can illuminate the clouds that often accumulate around larger matters and can reveal highlights and shadows often overlooked. This attack suggests that the pastoral mode is appropriate for the adolescent mind, with its intimations of importance and its illusions of power, whose weakness has not been toughened by repeated struggles with power outside its own consciousness. Its softness is fatal when called upon to engage oppression, tyranny, or injustice. According to this accusation, the pastoral is too easy, too accessible, and therefore a purveyor of false hopes to the shallow and undisciplined.

The last attack on the pastoral takes it at face value and says that all this pretentious discussion is not, in fact, grounded in the poem or in the poet's mind, at all, but is a tortured imposition on a delicate mode properly used for diversion. It is useful as a momentary escape and should not be restructured or compromised by a too-learned analysis. The pastoral is a bauble whose shine and color are entertaining at best and escapist at worst. For those who subscribe to the "life is real, life is earnest" view of the proper pursuit of existence, such diversion is tolerable only if everyone knows it is totally unrelated to the important matters of life. Such an attitude distrusts metaphor or poetry altogether except in so far as it is quarantined in a party atmosphere. Aspirations to plain speech protect against illusion, it is hoped. The pastoral poet knows that, but he also knows he is only a visitor to a garden that he himself laid out.

The escape to the countryside from the court or the metropolis is not made with a cart loaded with all earthly belongings; it is not desertion. The pastoral departure is more like a picnic; it is for a while. The journey is made to the hill across the river from the city where one gains a new perspective by looking back. To arrive at the hill and persist in looking away is to lose the contrast, the tension that lies just below the surface of pastoral poetry. Such avoidance produces only a flaccid wishfulness that cannot satisfy for very long.

The pastoral form can set up the traditional polarities between society and nature and between nature and art. It seems to base itself on the spontaneous rather than the planned, the direct rather than the subtle; the simple rather than the sophisticated, the native rather than the foreign. Such an understanding is possible if one looks only at the poem itself and what it says. The resulting estimation fulfills the need for escape brought to the poem by the reader. Within a larger frame of reference, the pastoral carries on another argument as well, an argument that calls such simplicities into question. Speaking with two voices is equivocation for some. It embodies the human condition for others.

COMPOSITIONS
OF POLITICS
AND MONEY

T he two literary gentlemen whose publications are the most extensive commentaries on the Picturesque, Richard Payne Knight and Uvedale Price, were both parliamentary supporters of the Whig alliance of the 1790s led by Charles James Fox. Whether that means that the Picturesque can be associated with a conservative or radical political attitude became the subject for some controversy after the recent exhibition and catalogue, *The Arrogant Connoisseur*, edited by Nicholas Penny and Michael Clark, focusing on Knight's multifaceted career. Because of their political alliance and because Price and Knight explicitly made a connection between aesthetic liberty and political liberty, the Picturesque has been given a political orientation. Only with the broadest of brushes could one attempt to depict the Picturesque as the Whig style. But the parallel compositions of government and sensory stimuli respond to the comparable challenge of exercising power while diffusing its effects. The proposal to take the association made between the two realms of aesthetics and politics more or less at face value, with full recognition that to do so sets aside a more critical reading of the rhetorical tactic that conflates the two realms, clearly points out the particular impetus of these essays. A compositional mode that cannot make a systematic case for itself in the face of more obviously controlled modes of selection is led to replicate its looser mixture of aesthetic stimuli as it argues around its irregular edges in search of supporting evidence.

Like the Picturesque, the Whigs were a mixed bunch. Only by radical pruning could the Whigs who opposed James II in the seventeenth century be made to line up with Joseph Addison,

Edmund Burke, and Charles James Fox of the eighteenth century. An answer to the question: What is a Whig? requires a host of qualifications comparable to the answer to the question: What is the Picturesque? And an attempt to clear the undergrowth in search of the essence of Whiggism, or, for that matter, the essence of the Picturesque, would leave us with barren ground. The following discussion of the Whigs, therefore, collects only those issues and attitudes that are useful in a discussion of the Picturesque. It does not presume to summarize the complex history of a political alliance. Certain attitudes toward exercising the power to compose the relationship of part to part and to a whole link politics and aesthetics. One is against absolute political power, the other is against an unmixed aesthetic system. They both prefer compositions built up from distinctive smaller parts combined and mixed together by means neither wholly rationalized nor completely random.

In addition to purely political events and allegiances surrounding their commentaries on aesthetics, when Price and Knight wrote about the Picturesque they employed a surprising number of political metaphors and references. Their work was taken in a political vein at the time as well and was attacked from politically partisan positions. The issues of mixture, contrast, and connection appear in both the aesthetic and the political realms. Events in the American colonies and in France focused attention on the displacement of despotism by liberty much as discussions of the strict arrangement of landscape features vied with freer compositions. Adjusting to changes in the relation between order and liberty was made more difficult by accelerating developments in the economic and technological conditions in late eighteenth-century England.

The political conditions surrounding the Picturesque are concurrent with the reign of George III. After the Whig ascendency in the first half of the eighteenth century, George III worked to frustrate, if not permanently contain, the political alignment dedicated to circumscribing royal influence. A hundred years earlier, the Whigs in the Glorious Revolution of 1688 had rallied around a political structure balanced between king, aristocracy, and people. By combining the virtues of monarchy, aristocracy, and democracy, the mixed constitution prevented the excesses of any one element from damaging the structure as a whole. Tyranny was the result of any pure form of power exercised without question or competition. Its singularity was dangerous not only to those who aspired to exercise an alternative power, but ultimately to itself. Despotism invited a violent replacement. The virtue of mixture was its resilience. The mixed constitution accepted perpetual tension and contention as the guarantee of a long life of partial control.

Mixture was seen as a potent force both to maintain one's own power and to diminish that of one's adversaries. Charles I had appealed to it as the insurer of balance. For others its most significant function was to check the corrupting effect of power. The concern that power exercised without challenge could only injure those holding it gave a rationale for the salutary effect of opposition. While aristocrats espoused mixture as a check on the centralization of royal power, it could equally be used by the crown to justify its corruption of Parliament by promises of preferment and position.

The Glorious Revolution had established a new relation between king and Parliament. After Parliament invited William of Orange to take the British throne in 1689, unchecked royal prerogative was dealt a fatal blow by the 1701 Act of Settlement that gave Parliament control of finances and the army. When Whigs were serving the court during the first half of the 1700s, they appealed to the arrangements of the Glorious Revolution as the source of political precedence. The "ancient constitution" of Anglo-Saxon times served as another source of Parliamentary independence, but it was a potentially uncontrollable one. The arrangements made by the Whigs in the Glorious Revolution were used to support the way things were while the ancient constitution justified periodic efforts to re-establish an imagined original condition. Having two sources for political justification allowed positions to be taken on almost any ground. Parliamentary power or constitutional principle were two possible motivations for Whig politicians. Those who shifted easily from one to the other were identifed as "trimmers." As is almost always the case when a politician is on the move, what you see may have nothing to do with what you get. Dissimulation is a venerable tactic to achieve ends one would rather not pursue openly. The Picturesque's use of deception can be easily confused with this political ploy.

While George III maneuvered to gain influence in Parliament by bestowing pensions and places in the royal network of patronage, radicals in the 1790s attempted to increase the influence of the people by making Parliament a more directly representative body. Such a proposal was met with little enthusiasm in the Commons because the members of Parliament did not wish to compromise their own freedom of action or dilute their discretion in exercising power. The members of Parliament were representatives, not delegates. They avoided attaching themselves to a doctrine that would establish direct lines of political power, either in the system as a whole or in their own particular branch of it. They argued that the virtue of the mixed constitution derived from its layers and displacements of directly expressed power. Although not so intricate as the system that Venice devised to prevent despotism in its oligarchy, eighteenth-century Britain enjoyed and defended its impure, mixed political structure. The radical opposition, who had no more love for a Whig oligarchy than for monarchy, charged the Whig leader Charles James Fox in 1783 with recommending the tyranny of Venice rather than the tyranny of France.

A balance was struck between protecting property and preserving liberty. Solid parliamentarians feared that a deluge of liberty would sweep away their property. The rule of law managed to contain such an assault by defining and limiting liberty. Taken from the radical position of pure ideals, all the adjustments, compromises, and exceptions that flowed from any balancing seemed to prove their nefarious intent. Taken as a pattern that permitted relatively easy adjustment of smaller parts to changing circumstances, dynamical balancing produced a marvelously flexible composition.

The Whig doctrine drew on the political theories that John Locke published immediately after the Glorious Revolution. His arguments in favor of liberty, resistance, sovereignty of the people, and the contract theory of the origin of civil government served the Whig aristocrats well until they themselves became accustomed to power. Comfortable positions rendered them less zealous for any ideals that sought to reopen the question of apportioning power. When they found themselves in opposition, however, many of the neglected principles vigorously reappeared.

Compromises with their own liberal heritage drew the Whig aristocrats closer to the traditional Tory identification with order and stability. Together they could be identified as the court party. Opposition to their program took the form of the country party consisting of the traditional power bases of the landed gentry who looked at political activity in London with a sideways glance. These noisy parliamentary back benchers, inheritors of the previous century's country alliance associated with Shaftesbury, interested in keeping as much autonomy and resources as possible at their local level, watched carefully over governmental expenditures that overwhelmingly depended on land taxes.

The scale of political and economic order was the country party's concern. As long as the centers of power were ultimately found in the great country houses and their lands, they were content. They resisted any scheme to strengthen the power structure centered in London, either by the king or by those hungry for alliances in Parliament. Because the country Whigs identified the established church, with the king at its head, as an arm of royal influence, the cause of the dissenters became an important expression for the liberal Whigs' resistance to royal power.

Although the continuous effort to thwart the exercise of authority by the crown could overreach itself and tip the balance in favor of uncontrolled liberty of the people, the country Whigs) feared tyranny more than they feared anarchy. Anarchy could be suppressed at a local scale; tyranny could not. Which evil seemed worse depended on the estimation of their relative strengths at any one time. Because of the Whigs' eternal distrust of the king, they moved into "formed and regular" opposition even at the cost of appearing treasonable or blindly hostile because they believed that occasional opposition could not exercise perpetual vigilance against the royal abuse of power. The resulting structure enshrined contest and a degree of roughness in recognition of the fact that the balance was a dynamical one.

The country party did not covet position and power at the court in London. Their world revolved around the stability of the land and the communities they dominated there. When they spoke of liberty, it was the ability to run their corner of the world more or less as they chose, free from courtly influence. Far more important to them was the protection of property. They regarded the intrigue at court as symptomatic of its parasitical dependence on rural virtues even as it perverted them. The country demonstrated the continuous, compact relationship of a whole world. The imagery conjured up by the country party took its place in a long tradition of rural virtue censuring courtly vice. The land received moral and economic power directly from the hand of the deity. It provided the bounty to sustain and ornament human life as well as provide a model of harmony and justice. Although the land was owned and exploited, it conferred the rectitude of its natural virtues on those operating in the neighborhood.

A whole segment of English literature was devoted to the legitimization of the latest families who had come into possession of the land. It was necessary to fabricate a mythology that made the present aristocrats of the land the ones most deserving of the position. Even their recent arrival, made possible by the most "unnatural" processes, did not prevent them from subsequently imagining themselves living according to the moral imperatives flowing from the land. Poetry celebrated the landed gentry as if they were as natural as the ancient trees, rocks, and streams they had just bought. A continuity was discovered, or created, between the source of virtue, the land, and the power that made use of it.

The country party repeatedly called for parliamentary reform, or rather, for controlling the number of Parliamentarians who owed their place or pension to the crown. The court party rejected such efforts at reform because they would make the House of Commons a body unmixed by crown influence and too purely a body of the people. This line of argument identifies a recurrent issue in politics as well as aesthetics: Must the mixture of forces be present at every scale of the composition? If the court party argued that while the Commons contributed to mixture at the scale of the nation as a whole, it should, within itself, be made up of the same contrasting elements, what kind of decentered composition is the result?

The country party felt that the balance between crown, aristocracy, and Commons was upset by the attempt to stack the benches with men who were not representatives of the people, but minions of the crown. The ancient constitution, to which they appealed, was based on the landowners' efforts to check the absolute power of the king. If their own power was being diluted by the application of mixture at the next smaller scale, they resisted with all the self-righteousness their vaunted principles could supply.

Less from reliance on Locke's sovereignty of the people argument, and more from the power conferred in fact and in the myth by the ancient constitution, the country party insisted that British government was based on the land: a familiar preindustrial argument. The power conferred by landownership was the only sure resistance to corruption emanating from the king. The Parliament could not act as a check to royal influence if it were not made up of men of substance. For this reason, parliamentary reform was not directed toward the ideal of universal suffrage. Such a radical idea would not provide sufficient resistance to concerted blandishments coming from the crown. The private gain represented by landownership was transformed into a public good providing the bulwark that protected the people from despotic or insidious royal influence.

At the same time that Parliament vigilantly protected its powers from encroachment by the crown, it kept direct contact from the people to a manageable level. Not only were there property requirements for membership in Parliament, but too frequent elections were resisted. An excess of changefulness in the membership would hamper steady resistance in this delicate mixture. The rise of party alignments, initially met with outrage from most quarters, served as a way to connect the separate interests of the opposition. Regular and formed opposition, which ideally should be reconstituted for every issue, much like the ideal picturesque composition, may have threatened the stability of the nation, but it was the only way to link the individual parts.

The most disturbing feature of the conditions in the last two decades of the eighteenth century for the country party was the rise of the money economy. The mobile, merely assigned rather than intrinsic, value of financial operations cut to the heart of the significance of the land. The court needed to be watched, not only because it was continuously trying to enlarge its power, but because it relied increasingly on the money-men in the City of London. The fact that most of the early steps toward industrialization came from men whose wealth was diverted from the land to iron, canals, roads, and factories did not cause the country party to rest any easier. It was precisely this transformation of land into money flowing into financial operations without location or stability that the country party viewed with great concern. As Adam Smith remarked, the great proprietors were seldom great improvers of the land. The merchants who became country gentlemen were generally the best of all improvers.

These decades have received considerable attention in the recent search for the conditions that lead to economic development by recognizing the critical changes that take place as patterns of

*this sense of
movement
underpins the
modern*

technology, finance, and production of wealth adapted to new potentials and conditions. The most characteristic change was in the scale of the activity. Everything seemed to be on the move: money, people, knowledge, materials. The cotton industry, which was such an important factor in industrialization, was the first large-scale economic activity to rely on a raw material that could not be domestically produced. Even on a regional scale, the economy was no longer a local, subsistence affair, but was developing into an integrated exchange structure as food and goods could be moved along the new and improved transportation lines.

The roads and canals were financed by local landowners who realized that larger markets and greater access to raw materials increased their worth. The resulting network was not thought about except in 20- to 50-mile increments. There was no regional, let alone national, plan guiding the effort. Such a pattern paralleled the seemingly random effect of innovation in other industrializing activities. Transportation produced a larger scale of mobility without anyone necessarily thinking of it in systematic terms. Laissez-faire seemed the most accurate explanation of the process. Because it was not rationalized at a large scale, these efforts could avoid responsibility or even awareness of some of the larger consequences of the revolution in transportation and industrialization. Incremental change obscured larger consequences and rendered them unintentional. Somehow a mixture of efforts produced a pattern, not quite a system, mind you, whose distinct parts could be made to work together.

Mobility threatened the traditional primacy bestowed on economic value derived from fixed location. The investment in roads and canals in these decades caught the imagination of the whole country and made connections between things as compelling as things themselves. Famine or surplus, savings or the need for credit were conditions whose effects could be distributed around the country by means of the growing transportation and financial networks. As an example of the dissolution of what had seemed

natural connections, in 1797 the Bank of England ended its obliga-
tion to convert its notes into gold. This severance of the link
between gold and the money supply, itself an advanced stage of
representation, to be sure, was a reaction to the shaken confidence
resulting from the need to import food and to prepare for armed
conflict with the unpredictable French Republic. The virtual disap-
pearance of gold and the substitution of banknotes and tradesmen's
tokens were evidence that the layers of represented value were
delaminating.

One of the disturbing consequences of the increase in economic scale for anyone who valued local conditions was the appearance of standards for production and financial arrangements. International trade required standardization precisely because direct
observation could not confirm the operations of production or
investment. These patterns of activity were not decided at the local
level, and because they were not natural forces like drought or
storm, the local community resented them. Somebody, but no one
the locals knew, was making decisions that they had to live with,
and over which they seemed to have no more control than of the
wind. Distrust of systematization was easily reinforced. The need to
have a voice in the process ("No taxation without representation!")
fired most of the radical appeals of the day.

The land itself began to lose some of its direct meaning. It was
no longer exclusively the source of individual metabolic survival.
The direct sustenance one could derive from it was overlaid by its
value to an absent landowner who interpreted it, not from direct
inspection exercised by those who live on it every day, but from an
indirect representation, usually in a London office. The land as a
producing resource was now thought of with reference to a national and international horizon. Returns on investment in draining
swamps and breeding livestock would not be realized until a later
season. Both time and place were being treated indirectly at a scale
heretofore unknown. Specialization of activity and the substitution

of scientific knowledge for tradition also broke the perceivable continuity of the immediate, local conditions.

The land was no longer the exclusive concern of those in direct, daily contact with it. George III, the government, the Board of Agriculture instituted in 1793, all took special interest in agriculture. This period of British history witnessed an acceleration in the evolution of the land from an organic whole, rooted and concentrated in unique locations, into a phenomenon whose meanings could be diffused far and wide. It remained as a perceivable "thing," yet it was now represented in many different ways, in many different places. The much discussed Enclosure Acts of Parliament after 1780 did not drive agricultural laborers en masse from the land to the factories. The initial effect was actually to upgrade the small-sized, occupying landowners. The stripping of the agricultural population did not gain momentum until the nineteenth century.

Land, as the traditional measure of status, retained its significance for those whose wealth flowed from trade or industrial products. They could buy it, improve it, and acquire a venerable patina in a much quicker fashion than had previous owners. Phyllis Dean's statement, "The most important achievement of the industrial revolution was that it converted the British economy from a wood-and-water basis to a coal-and-iron basis," alerts us to a change in the meaning of trees and rivers. With the shortage of timber an increasing reality for construction, leading to a substitution of stone and brick, trees became objects of contemplation for more than their board-foot content. Organic, natural systems were displaced by industrial and aesthetic ones.

The early stages of British industrialization produced a pattern of small points of investment supported by local agricultural wealth and local banks that eventually aggregated, without a rationalized plan, into a "system" of economic and labor activity. Adam Smith characterized that pattern as guided by an "invisible hand." That is an unfortunate image because it reinforces the suspicion that behind the scenes someone is, in fact, controlling everything. By not being explicit, the connection of various singular events is open to the charge of manipulation. The fear of behind-the-scene manipulation can also easily be attached to any illusions called "pictures." The represented scene is designed to create the desired effect through words, gestures, and costumes while the machinery is hidden backstage. The laissez-faire doctrine associated with those who look like they are doing nothing while, in fact, they are arranging everything arouses the same suspicion with regard to the Picturesque.

A distinction could be made between "natural" and "artificial" economics. Either term could be interpreted in a positive way, but tradition gave prominence to economic activity based on the land. The competition between artifice and nature surfaced on many fronts, not the least of which was the status of a tree.

The accumulation of capital through savings is one form of doing less at a given moment than one could. It withholds power in order to expend it at a later time. This practice, much admired by various dissenting protestants, led to an outward simplicity of life that masked an increasingly powerful economic status. A free-flowing stream is one thing; a dammed one channeled to a waterfall is another. Before the use of the steam engine (water significantly removed from its "natural" condition), dams were used to control floods, to provide power for grinding and spinning as well as to give the land an aesthetic composition. Of course downstream from a dam it is difficult to tell if the water tumbling over the rocks was always free or whether, at one time, it submitted to artificial containment.

The most direct connection between the commentators on the Picturesque and the Whigs was the large, swarthy form of Charles James Fox. His political career demonstrates the mixture and abrupt variation one associates with the new aesthetic mode. After entering Parliament in 1767, a seat which he took up after returning from Europe with his Eton schoolmate Uvedale Price, he allied himself by 1776 with the Rockingham Whigs, a faction that had taken up the country party program. Before his father's death in 1774, Charles had followed the court Whig leanings of his family, supporting the crown with its abhorrence of opposition and a disdain for opinion that originated outside Parliament. Charles James Fox's eventual identification with the Rockingham Whigs took several years to be confirmed and coincided with his election from Westminster, the populous and radical constituency in London.

The large landowners constituting this opposition group were not enthusiastic politicians. They preferred the enjoyment of country diversions and wagering on horse racing in which Fox enthusiastically joined and disastrously lost. Edmund Burke, who later split with Fox on the implications of the French Revolution, was secretary to Lord Rockingham and vainly tried to channel the faction's desultory political preferences into reasoned argument. His desire to earn a place in the charmed circle of the great Whig lords ignited his brilliant rhetoric in the service of their more languid heads. Fox identified with Rockingham, who reserved endorsements of any exclusive political structure by arguing for the mixed constitution in the clearest terms in the revival of debate on reform in 1790: "I can no more consent to let the Aristocratical Part preponderate over the Democratical than I can suffer the influence of the Crown to endanger the other two."

Charles James Fox came to politics with the background of his father's attempts at parliamentary leadership at mid-century. Henry Fox had managed to lose the race for position when he was passed over by events that his rival William Pitt the Elder seized and turned to his advantage. Fox salvaged total loss by gaining the appointment to the paymaster office in 1755, a position that compensated for its lack of political power by the opportunity it afforded to make money. The standing army, one of the thorns in the Whig ideologues' side, received a yearly allocation from Parliament. The paymaster oversaw this considerable sum and paid it out as needed. In the meantime he could use the remainder in various schemes whose return was all his. Like so many newly rich, the elder Fox eventually augmented his London estate of Holland House by the purchase of a rural homestead at Kingsgate, north of Dover, which was considered to have been built in imitation of Cicero's Formian villa on the coast of Baiæ. This first-generation Fox-Pitt competition extended to the second generation as Pitt the Younger contested parliamentary power with Charles James Fox in the 1790s.

Charles James Fox is an endearing and frustrating political figure. He became a man of principle through human enthusiasm rather than through careful construction. He was beloved by his friends and dismissed by his enemies for his unstable mix of political principle and political maneuvering. The younger Fox, in part from his youthful penchant for gambling, inherited the suspicion attached to sharp financial dealing that had made his father's fortune. And yet in 1793, by which time he had become the obvious standard-bearer of the liberal traditions of the Whigs, his financial embarrassments were removed by a group of aristocratic friends, not all of whom subscribed to his political leanings, who collected funds to clear his debts and set up an annuity.

Fox's career invites the partiality of narrow dismissal as well as broad adulation. One can go too far in trying to solidify his various positions and reversals into an arguable system. Yet there is something compelling about his brilliant arguments in Parliament even in the imperfect transcriptions made on the spot. Reports from those who heard Fox were unanimous in their judgment that he was the finest orator of the age. Such an honor is, however, a fugitive estimation. So much depends on the moment. And the wise comment made on Fox's death that he was greatest in reply rather than in proposal reinforces the dependent nature of his stature. Fox's oratory drew attention very early. If not in his maiden speech in 1769, then shortly thereafter, the quickness of his mind coupled with a compression of meaning and a fertility of imagination astonished his parliamentary colleagues. His speeches were judged to be "teeming with thought and overflowing with a torrent of ideas." Polish and balance were not characteristic of his orations; rather, "In him we beheld the massy materials of the scarcely finished structure, the rough but masterly specimens of the sculptor's art." This estimation from the *Morning Post* on Fox's death captures in visual terms the impact his words had on the ear and the mind. The readiness to make a visual analogy may indicate how close were the patterns of picturesque composition and political style.

The memorable issues that Fox came to speak out on as the leader of liberal-leaning Whigs all extended the ideal of liberty. After some uncertainty during the American Revolution, he came to support the rights of the English colonists. His support of the French Revolution, of course, caused him the greatest pain. But he spoke out forcefully in favor of Catholic emancipation, the end of slavery, and parliamentary reform. At the December 1792 meeting of the Whig Club of England, which had been formed by the more liberal members of the party after the 1784 electoral debacle that decimated the ranks of Fox's followers, Fox's toasts confirmed his support of liberty: "Equal Liberty to all Mankind" and "Rights of the People." Such statements are not to be read without remembering the parallel belief that some are more equal than others in terms of their participation in the mixed government of Britain. Having said that, however, is not to have said that the toast was mere dissimulation. Sorting out the interaction between these two positions is one of the bracing challenges of thinking with Fox and his Whig followers.

The 1784 electoral defeat meant that the Rockingham Whigs reluctantly turned away from the broadly complacent centers of the great Whig families and focused on a leaner constituency whose wealth depended more on trading and smaller estates and whose interest in reform shaded uncomfortably close to radicalism. Fox was less reluctant than many others in Parliament and his efforts to keep both the Whig lords and the reformers together ultimately proved unsuccessful. He could not find the connection that would subsume the parts to a whole. It seemed that his own peculiar political constitution was the only integrating force.

Parliamentary reform is an issue that most clearly brings out the complexity of the Whig political position. The contest for power between the crown and Parliament gave the Whigs a principled reason to work against dominance by the executive power. They had defined themselves on this issue in the seventeenth century. In the later decades of the eighteenth century, the matter had taken on new facets. Party, as a persisting alliance, came to be justified as the only reliable authority to resist pressure from the king. By 1783, with the events in France causing concern over what could happen if the crown were fatally disabled, Fox was making claims for the House of Commons that troubled conservatives. By suggesting that the crown was a threat to constitutional liberty more serious than that posed by Thomas Paine's radicals or even by the French Revolution, he seemed to align with the radical position. The reformers, however, could not trust Fox because his previous actions seemed to suggest that his vaunted ideals were nothing more than an "aristocratic plot." And yet, Fox was always attuned to the concentration of power in the hands of an executive body, whether king or Robespierre. He congratulated his nephew on "that parallel you drew between the Jacobins of France and the Crown party here." His sympathies were not blind.

The radical call for universal suffrage entailed some compromises to the ideal of the mixed constitution that Fox and other Whigs could not support. Fox's reasons for preserving the indirect structure seem prescient in our world of twenty-second television "bites." "His objection to universal suffrage was not distrust of the decision of the majority, but because there was no practical mode of collecting it." Any attempt to collect it would, through "the operation of hope on some, fear on others, and all the sinister means of influence that would so certainly be exerted," result in "fewer individual opinions" than an "appeal to a limited number." The clear motivation for this position is the preservation of a range of opinions. The mixture of sufficiently powerful interests was the only defense against the focusing of power in a singular position or binary opposition. The "natural princes" would vigilantly watch each other to prevent any peremptory move to dominate. Their proposals for electoral reform were designed to preserve their legitimate leadership. The range of interests expressed by such a mixture would be much greater than a vast number of smaller interests that could only be aggregated by allegiance to very simplified propositions.

Fox's belief in mixture is justifiable only because he did not abstract power into a monolithic category uniting all who possessed it into a conspiracy of self-preservation. Such an abstraction cannot make the discrimination that Fox made in the struggles for power between those who had less and those who had more. These struggles kept tyranny at bay. The ideal of preserving mixture lies at the heart of Fox's political life. For him simplifying abstractions were despotic. Only constant effort would keep political circumstances from congealing in an entropic singularity. Universal suffrage exercised choice at every individual point in the political structure. Such dispersion of choice could be perverted by centers of power that manipulated groups who could exercise their power only in isolated, singular acts. Such centers could mask their manipulation by appealing to the rights of individuals even as they shamelessly suppressed them.

Fox was always distrusted by the Whig lords who could not follow his apparent radicalism and by the reformers because he kept stopping short of their ultimate goals. He avoided a revolutionary dinner on July 14, 1791, so as not to lose the support of the Whig grandees. When the Association of the Friends of the People was founded in 1792 by his eager young followers, he tried to keep their parliamentary reform efforts at a distance in order not to alarm the Whig establishment led by the Duke of Portland. Fox was torn between these opposing alliances of friends largely because he interpreted the contemporary conflicts as further manifestations of the old opposition between crown and Parliament. Portland saw the defeat of the Whigs by Mr. Pitt the Younger in 1784 as a serious injury to the natural leadership of the aristocracy. Fox, trapped by earlier conventions, missed the gravity of this shift on a larger scale and saw it instead as an "assault on the priviledges of the Commons." His sensitivity to a certain configuration of political issues was extremely acute. He defined it and argued it with great energy. The stresses inherent in his position gave it vitality and can be interpreted as an unsuccessful effort to grapple with the forces constituting a new composition. That he could not step to the next level of evaluation may indicate that the balance between movement and stasis is much more difficult than we, and certainly he, believed.

Fox's response to the established church reveals his perpetual fear of tyranny. He was convinced that toleration and moderate behavior, the optimum characteristics of a civil society, would be the salutary result of members of the Church "being forced to hear the arguments of the Dissenters; by their being obliged to oppose argument to argument." The intermingling of thought produced by such discussion would establish liberty for all concerned. Without such exchange, the Church could impose "the silence of the strong hand of power." This silence, opaque, unresponsive, tyrannical, expressed power directly, unmediatedly. It did not stoop to explanations or representations. By breaking into communicable pieces through listening and talking, power may risk losing position, but, and this is the important part, it actually prolongs a position. Fox wrote to his parliamentary leader the Marquis of Rockingham in 1779 that it was his opinion that "power (whether over a people or a king) obtained by . . . degrees, rather than by a sudden exertion of strength, is in its nature more durable and firm." For the members of the established church to break into speech requires "that modest confidence in the truth of their own tenet, and charity for those of others." Another level of belief, beyond the point under discussion, is preserved in the assumption that both the established church and the Dissenters are working from the same principles. This faith in the shared realm, which underlay Fox's most radical calls for liberty, is the kind of indissoluble connection that replaces any singly focused, systematic political structure.

Belief in a shared realm suggested that differences separating religious or political parties lie on the visible surface. One is not to take those differences as the whole truth. Fox argued that the Test Act, which required profession of faith in the Church of England as a prerequisite for participation in political life, produced surfaces that looked the same, but could conceal differences in the actual belief behind the oath. The Test Act invited dissembling and produced the form of worship without its substance. Enforced similarity of form could conceal fatal differences, whereas differences in outward form could actually arise from a common belief. Waiting for people's actions before judging them is preferable to collecting "the evidence of your future conduct, from what I know to be your opinions. . . . Men ought to be judged by their actions, and not by their thoughts." The emphasis is on close attention to what happens, what is present, not to invisible patterns of thought, generalized and abstracted. Such a potentially disconnected or atomized procedure seems to resist attempts at establishing connections between discrete facts. For Fox such a connection did exist. He took it as a given in the religious and political setting of eighteenth-century Britain, but he did not trouble himself to give it more than a vague outline.

The status of theory in relation to practice is also implicated by such a conception. Fox was no theoretician. It was the sparkle and movement of the passing forms that took all his attention. The rapid responses of his fertile mind were not derived from theoretical calculation, but from the urging of immediate human contact. His belief in the "collision of opinions, in open and liberal discussion" was much greater than his belief in principle driven by the cold mechanics of theory. In response to Pitt the Younger's motion for reform in Parliament in May 1783, Fox expressed his allegiance in the clearest terms: The "nature of our Constitution required innovation and renovation; for the beauty of the Constitution did not consist, as some people imagined, in theory, but in practice." Local events took precedence over abstract concepts.

Fox's split with Edmund Burke illustrates this habit of thought most vividly. They had begun their close political association in 1774 by speaking out against the government's handling of the American colonial war and had worked together in the Rockingham circle of Whigs. But when the French Revolution, initially greeted with sympathy by both men, had taken a violent turn, Burke's fear of anarchy got the better of him. His "Reflections on the Revolution in France" appeared in 1790. Fox knew that Burke's pamphlet would split the Whig opposition, led by the Duke of Portland, and give comfort to the government led by William Pitt the Younger. In the course of a debate on another matter of foreign affairs, Burke, consumed by the need to crush the French heresy, diverted to attack the Rights of Man and other French excesses. He was harried by comments coming from Fox's Whig supporters and from Fox himself, who took issue on a point of order whether such matters were germane to the question before the House. Burke could take no more and, overcome by zealous righteousness, rejected Fox's whispered appeal to friendship and declared "their friendship was over."

Fox could not believe his ears. "Tears trickled down his cheeks, and he strove in vain to give utterance that dignified and exalted his nature." Fox's political motivations were built on a deep foundation of affection for the individual presence of his friends. For Burke, master of dressing abstract principle in colorful detail, the principle could not be sacrificed to the individual. As Fox believed in the underlying virtue of those who loved liberty in France, he also believed in the underlying affection that sustained friendship. Differences that appeared on the surface could be over-looked. Burke, despite his lifelong effort to solidify his position by

[handwritten marginal note: aesthetic parallel here]

putting powerful arguments at the service of those who were born to participate in government, finally could not abide their complacent habits. Specifically Fox's picturesquely unplanned tactics drew his ire: "As to any plan of conduct in our own Leaders there are not the faintest Traces of it—nor does it seem to occur to them that any such thing is necessary. Accordingly everything is left to accidents."

Fox's explicit connection to the Picturesque is not great, as far as the record tells. He maintained his friendship with his schoolmate Uvedale Price and knew Payne Knight well enough to refer to him in a letter to his longtime friend and political ally Richard Fitzpatrick in December 1798: "Price writes to me to recommend some plays and he mentions Knight's opinion of them, but not yours." The letter was written from the country cottage, St. Anne's Hill, which Fox had bought in 1784. The picture of the house and descriptions of the grounds are not so extreme in their composition as to serve as a characteristically picturesque example. Its modesty encompassed simple comfort to a degree that would not seem to have made it a demonstration of any aesthetic mode. His neighbor, Charles Hamilton of Painshill, may have been consulted in the embellishment of St. Anne's Hill. Fox was aware of the discussions surrounding that new mode as his comment in a letter in July 1801 makes clear: "Virgil is more beautiful to be sure; but yet by being more general he is less picturesque or (since Price has given such a fanciful meaning to the word) I suppose I must say less descriptive." Fox sat with Price and Knight at a dinner at the Royal Academy and discussed poetry and art with Knight at Whitehall in 1796.

These scattered references do not either prove or disprove much of anything beyond Fox's awareness of the Picturesque. What is important here is Fox's belief in liberty even when it did not advance his career.

Charles James Fox was even drawn into the political implications of pastoralism when he received an appeal from the poet William Wordsworth in 1801 regarding the charges that his poem "Michael" was a danger to the kingdom because it could incite the small farmers to resistance. Wordsworth assured Fox that it had no economic implication from his point of view; that it was art, not politics. The year before, William Windham had worried in the House of Commons about a comparable impact of Robert Bloomfield's "Farmer's Boy," which had been published with a preface by a leading radical, Capell Lofft.

The evolution of the pastoral and the Picturesque into explicitly political matters is an interpretation loaded with social significance, quite apart from the evolution toward ornamental dreaming. The pastoral and the Picturesque can be arranged either to serve as revolutionary or counterrevolutionary phenomena. This two-facedness, displacing the status of the matter into a continual dialogue, is one of the problematical and essential characteristics of both modes.

The liberty that Fox stood for lay between tyranny on one side and license on the other. As circumstances shifted, so did the appeals to liberty. What at one time seemed an excuse for tyranny, at another seemed justifiable protection from license. The pastoral also seemed to shift inexplicably between calls for artifice and nature, emphasizing one over the other by turns and the Picturesque appeared as an indistinct category situated between the Beautiful and the Sublime.

The Picturesque sought to understand a particular set of circumstances in the economic and political development of late eighteenth-century Britain. It looked both backward and forward. When it argued for the preservation of some ballast in the operation of society, it found the weight in the provincial power centers of the aristocratic landowners. They prevented the whole nation from rushing off in a million different directions. At the same time the Picturesque worked against the formation of a single power center. The clear boundary of the island became the "whole" that must not be allowed to be a unitary site of tyranny. On the other hand multiple centers of organization distributed across the land could not drift away completely in a fit of independence.

The liberty admired by the advocates of the Picturesque applied to the scale of these subcenters. To break the composition down any further was to risk disintegration. The increase in the circulation of goods, people, and money worked against any simple despotism, but if allowed to proceed on an open plane, it would produce no recognizable pattern whatsoever. And some idea of recognizable pattern haunted the Picturesque aesthetic. Its tolerance for ambiguously organized compositions was newly acquired so it is not suprising that their arguments slipped periodically back into an earlier ideal of formality. But their effort to become adept at making and appreciating a newer, more free-form arrangement did not extend to their political musings. Almost as if the advocates of the Picturesque understood how dependent it is on some concentration of means, they could not recommend any change that would disperse the pattern of political and economic concentration from which they benefitted.

This conflict is an irreducible one for the Picturesque. Ultimately the freedom to experiment with increasingly loosened aesthetic compositions seems constrained by a political and economic pattern that is less so. Without the concentrated weight of such an anchor, it was feared that the whole thing would fly apart. The implications of the aesthetic Picturesque could not quite be permitted in the political realm. Once again we see the Picturesque trembling between freedom and order, the uncomfortable middle position equally open to attack from both sides.

LIBERTY
NOT LICENSE

When writers on the Picturesque discussed aesthetic matters, they repeatedly used political metaphors, and when they discussed politics, they used metaphors from landscape design. As members of Parliament, or of the stratum of society from which parliamentarians came, they lived in a world suffused with politics. In the later years of the eighteenth century, political issues were very much in the forefront of their attention, and the language of politics came easily to tongue or pen. Metaphors that linked political thought to other realms of activity were not, therefore, unique in discussions at the time. For example, when Payne Knight's poem *The Landscape* was reviewed in the *Critical Review* in July 1795, the author commented that "the poem concludes—as most poems we have read of late do conclude—with the French Revolution."

The use of political metaphors in discussions of landscape design may go beyond a fashionable turn of phrase or a rhetorical ploy. A common thread can be spun to connect the use of power in aesthetic as well as political modes. A three-termed characterization of the way power is exercised ranged from tyranny on one end, to license on the other. At these extremes the exercise of power was either obvious and uniform or loose and erratic. A position somewhere between the two avoided the excesses of both. The middle term is liberty, a continuously negotiated balance asserting obvious power when license seemed in the ascendent and loosening the rules when tyranny appeared as a threat. The appearance of a middle term between two opposing political categories brings to mind the middle term of the Picturesque inserted between Edmund Burke's categories of the Beautiful and the Sublime.

[handwritten annotation: how many uses of this term are there in 18th + 19th c.]

For Uvedale Price, landscape design and government were aspects of a common activity he identified as "improvement." The salient issue in each was how to exercise the means to achieve the desired result. In both cases, Price, the Foxite Whig, is most concerned that sufficient natural freedom be allowed. Not unexpectedly, however, he is quick to note that neither "improvers nor legislators will leave everything to neglect and accident." Preparing for future changes and their effects on society as well as gardens suggests that improvers and legislators will act so as "not to suppress the workings of nature, but to watch, and take indications from them; for who would choose to settle in that place, or under that government, where the warnings, indications, and all the free efforts of nature, were forcibly counteracted and suppressed?" The watchfulness required to engage successfully in either government or gardening brings to mind the warning that the price of liberty is eternal vigilance.

Landscape despotism was represented by the large-scale depredations perpetrated by Price and Knight's least favorite gardener and most favorite target: Lancelot Brown, he of the "Capability" sobriquet. Price's parody of Brown, having him say: "You shall never wander from my walks—never exercise your own taste and judgment—never form your own compositions—neither your eyes nor your feet will be allowed to stray from the boundaries I have traced," sets up a political comment that such tyranny is "a species of thralldom unfit for a free country." The Brownians' control of experience reaches military intensity as it lays the ground open as if to prevent an ambuscade from intruders or enemies. The leveling of ground, houses, orchards, gardens, all of which are swept away, opens for display a "dreary selfish pride" wishing to reign alone. It suppresses "variety, amusement and humanity" in favor of despotic monotony.

Brown's landscape art lay firmly in the line of evolution toward "naturalness" begun by the likes of Lord Burlington, Addison, and Pope in the early years of the eighteenth century. His clumps, belts, and serpentine waters were a long way from French or Dutch geometric formality in their appearance, if not in their systematic application. When the Picturesque, represented by Price, comes along and regrets the replacement of one style by another, anyone who had loyally carried on the struggle to overcome the hegemony of geometry could hardly be blamed for feeling betrayed. As Price recognized: "I shall probably be accused by Mr. Brown's admirers, of endeavouring to bring about a counter-revolution, and to restore the ancien-regime, with all its despotism of straight lines and perpetual symmetry. It is true that I have some attachment to the old monarchy, though I should not like to have it restored without strict limitations; but my wish, in this instance, is to combat the despotism of the modern improver." The most powerful means to combat systematic despotism was vigilantly to maintain a mix of contrasts and irritations.

The effect of the Glorious Revolution of 1688, so revered by the Whigs in the eighteenth century, may have introduced a taste for a more responsive and "natural" exercise of power over people as well as trees, but Price used William of Orange's arrival as the parallel for a garden art characterized by its "steady, considerate, and connected arrangement." Both gardens and government were "equally free from the blind prejudice for antiquity; and rage for novelty; neither fond of destroying old, nor of creating new systems."

Revolutionaries who wished to supplant one pure system by another were incipient despots no different from the present despots of the dominant system. Following the regret Price felt after destroying the "old-fashioned" garden in his youth, he went on to explain his excesses by comparing himself to "a man of careless, unreflecting, unfeeling good-nature, [who] thought it his duty to vote for demolishing towns, provinces, and their inhabitants, in America." The general, but not unanimous, support for the war against the American colonists was goaded on by "the blind, unrelenting power of system." No conciliatory methods that would have produced a mixture of principles were tried, the opposition was thrown down and destroyed.

The level openness ascribed to the Brownian "system" had the effect of reducing the fear of the unknown. In his gardens one had no trouble seeing what one was getting. Their obviousness was reassuring to those still not quite convinced either of their own grip on social position or of their grasp of the latest fashion. The excitement of picturesque mystery becomes threatening to the timid or the worried.

Uvedale Price and Richard Payne Knight both wrote on explicitly political matters in addition to their commentaries on the Picturesque. The conservatism of their social and economic positions has come through quite clearly to some observers. Price's "Thoughts on the Defense of Property," published in 1797, supported the traditional conviction of property holders that property, concentrated like the ballast of a ship, was the surest defense against the excesses of license. "Property inspires a love of order, and a dread of confusion," is how he put it. The ideal condition of the British society derived from the pattern of property distribution and the way that wealth circulated within that pattern. The distribution was marked by many levels of gradation. These gradations "are all equally secured, and equally favoured by the laws." The way that these levels connected to one another, the communication between the highest and lowest, was "less separated by the pride of rank or fortune, than in any other kingdom."

Price is not describing anything like an even distribution. There clearly are differences, but the gradation between them is sufficiently close to make it seem a continuity rather than a chasm, when viewed from the proper distance. As a country member of Parliament, Price felt close to the yeoman and suspicious of the "profligate and desperate men of a great metropolis." "Ambition destroys local attachments," is how he sought to establish the virtues of the land over the temptations of trade. Property was rooted in a place on the earth; it was ballast, not sail. Keeping the parts of society attached to each other, in a whole body, kept Britain from falling apart as France had.

The fear that somehow the enthusiasms of individual rights would overwhelm the British monarchy stimulated Price to write this little treatise. He was not unaware of the discontent that could arise from those at the lowest level of property distribution. His concern for the laboring poor was less for their own welfare than for the stability of the system whose dissolution would be very painful for him. "I trust that such will be the effect of our union, and that it will be shewn by a general and encreased attention to the welfare of that most useful and necessary body of men—the laborers; for without their genuine attachment, however firmly we may be united to each other, our union would be far from complete." By giving them some stake, or its appearance, in the continuity of society, they will defend it from attack.

Richard Payne Knight wrote a poem on the death of his parliamentary leader, Charles James Fox, in 1806. In it the political shades of Knight's thought are more explicit, despite the encomium's adulatory tone. Fox, according to Knight, displayed quickness in detecting "metaphysic fallacies" while exercising his intuitive grasp of the truth that lay behind external forms. In the midst of the changes confronting England, hope rather than despair was possible because Fox had been able to resist "all the cold narcotic lore / Which reason spreads where fancy loves to soar." Fox's warm heart linked to a lively intellect provided him with the two powers required for a statesman. Those who take up the metaphysical posture discount immediate facts which the heart knows, while those "wise in forms" lose sight of the larger end that the intellect perceives. Fox was a mixture of both. Knight elevates Fox to the powerful middle position. He possessed both the "Statesman's wisdom" and the "Patriot's vigor." Fox is confined "to no sect's or party's views," but moves freely as the ideal and the situation demand. For some partisans who contended with him, this description, unintentionally, recalled Fox's opportunism in the pursuit of position. The most memorable was his attachment to Lord North's parliamentary coalition only months after making bitter attacks on North. When Knight freely characterized the Picturesque as promiscuous, he might also have been describing Fox's indiscriminate large-heartedness.

The ability to see beyond the forms allows Fox to detect what would currently be called "trends." Knight identifies an interest in innovation as one of Fox's important political senses. Others may dread it, and be trapped into pursuing "the beaten track," but Fox looks up from familiar forms and notices that "all around is new." It is not immediately clear whether this is a conservative posture or not.

The central characteristic of the Picturesque is the exercise of less control than one has access to. Although Knight asserts the fact that Fox was "Above the trick of Art," he glowingly describes how the "Statesman's sense assumed the Courtier's ease." By citing Castiglione's recommendation to display *sprezzatura*, or less concern and labor than is, in fact, present, Knight reminds us how deep are the roots of the tradition of living beneath one's means. As Castiglione recommended, particularly in the acquisition of musical skill, the Courtier is to conceal the effort he expended learning to play the lute, and, when called upon to join in musical activities, is to play with intentional lapses in perfection. By seeming not to have the skill under systematic control, everyone is put at ease and can enjoy themselves more completely. Knight paints a Machiavellian picture of Fox that shows him "careful with lessers." By addressing them in lowered tones, free of any immodesty, without pomp or sarcastic wit, the statesman establishes the connection required between the levels of a civil society. In his pursuit of "universal good," Fox was guided by "Truth undisguised," and whatever adornment truth might wear is confined to "native charms."

The Picturesque emphasized immediate sensory stimulus to correct a dominant aesthetic mode that seemed to rely on abstract, intellectual structures. The nature/artifice contrast is partly about the relation between these two factors in aesthetic speculation. A comparable emphasis on present details, in contrast to abstract structures, appears in Fox's discussion of parliamentary representation to the electors of Westminster. He "stressed the insufficiency of an abstract opportunity. Having the office of Parliamentary representative for yourselves is only the beginning of the matter. The specifics of who holds that office makes all the difference . . . [I]t is still necessary that you should attend to the use of that instrument, and watch vigilantly that it be placed in proper hands." Vigilance is not necessary for situations that are set up, grasped all at once, and referred to subsequently in the abstract. It is required for changing conditions needing constant attention to pick up irregularities and variations.

The politicized atmosphere in which the Picturesque was being argued is evident in Horace Walpole's attack on Knight in a 1796 letter to his co-conspirator in the controversy, George Mason, whose *Essay on Design in Gardening* had been greatly revised in the previous year to include attacks on Price and Knight. Walpole and Mason's orientation descended from the mid-century Whigs whose parliamentary dominance had clearly made them part of the court rather than the country party. Mixing political and aesthetical metaphors, Walpole accused Knight of being one who "Jacobinically would level the purity of gardens" and in the same spirit "would as malignantly as Tom Paine or Priestley guillotine Mr. Brown." The serious distortion in this charge is the assumption that the Picturesque was being recommended as a revolutionary replacement rather than a salutary mixture. Walpole was not alone in levelling the political charge. A proper aristocratic lady, Anna Seward, commented shortly after *The Landscape* was published that "Knight's system appears to me the Jacobinism of taste."

In the face of disturbing events across the Channel and the fear that the contagion of the French Revolution might take hold in Britain, more conservative elements looked for opportunities to display patriotic fervor even through advocating a particular landscape design. Price recognized this motive in Walpole's and Mason's praises for English gardening, but he knew how such narrow partisanship limited their comprehension of the more complex issues he was espousing. He sought to blunt their invidious charge that his criticism of some aspects of current English landscape improvement was unpatriotic by saying: "My love for my country is, I trust, not less ardent than theirs, but it has taken a different turn; and I feel anxious to free it from the disgrace of propagating a system." His desire, consistent with all that these comments have suggested, was for "a more liberal and extended ideal of improvement to prevail."

The attacks on the Picturesque for its political implications were stirred by the winds of partisanship. In such an atmosphere, the intrinsic issues on which the advocates of the Picturesque wished to concentrate were lost. Attacked from all sides, Price remonstrated: "He who expresses warmly his love of freedom, and hatred of despotism—however carefully he may distinguish freedom from licentiousness, and despotism from limited monarchy — must never hope for candor. He will be treated by zealots, as a friend of anarchy and confusion, as an enemy to all order and regularity, as one who would wish to see mankind in what is called a state of nature."

Nature becomes the anchor in a storm of trade and the immoderate expansion of civilization. The Picturesque was seen by some who wished to take it straight as a way to govern license. Using nature as a model, they reattached improvement to a stable and certain rule. Liberty also gained adherents who saw it as the way for genuine social patterns to replace the distortions of despotism. Conversely, the Picturesque was seen as dangerous deception using the appearance of nature to perpetrate a lie. Liberty was also attacked because when it loosened sacred social bonds, it unleashed a flood of licentious selfishness. Trying to fend off these two opposing factions made writing about the Picturesque a strenuous and confusing task.

The only acceptable way for power or control to be exercised was reluctantly. One of the early examples of a more naturalistic garden design filled with emblematic views complete with seats and tablets presenting poetical sentiments, was William Shenstone's Leasowes, 25 miles east of Knight's Downton Castle. Quotations from Virgil, Horace, and Pope and statues of Pan and Venus led one around a course to scenes and vistas improved by the gardener's hand. William Shenstone, a poet who published a "Pastoral Ballad" in the December 1751 *London Magazine*, considered artifice, or "sweet concealment," a natural part of the gardener's art. The parts of a composition had to be brought together and their relationship adjusted in order to create beauty. As far as the formerly independent parts were concerned, this exercise of power was "coercive." Such a tyrannical, if necessary, act could escape censure only if the coercive chain was intertwined reluctantly. Beauty, by declining to rule as a sovereign, "best deserves to reign." Rather than seizing the opportunity to exercise power directly, eagerly, it is preferable to withhold such open action, to work unseen, coyly, and with reservation.

The effort to find a balance between the slow and certain repetitions of natural country life and the energy and change of the city appears in discussions of politics and aesthetics. In a novel *Village Memoires* (1775) written as a series of letters between a village clergyman and his city-dwelling son, Joseph Craddock sums up the argument when he observes that, while a man's sensibility is worn out and made infirm by perpetual motion on "the ocean of life," it becomes contracted and despondent when it is confined in the solitude of "an unextended empire." Staying at home where power and resources are easily correlated to immediate domestic requirements must be balanced with the "restless pursuit of some hidden good." This conservative position is far from enjoying the mystery of concealed effects in a picturesque composition. The leveling effect of "turnpike-roads and circulating libraries [that] are the great inlets of vice and debauchery" could also be found in the realities of the current political scene. "The man who bids fairest for success, as candidate for any office where the public is principally concerned, is not he who has the most friends, but he who has the fewest enemies—not he whose talents raise an idea of superiority, but he whose mediocrity begets respect." The reliable connection of means and ends, of admirable effects rising from virtuous intentions, seems utterly severed.

Even garden art attending to the "genius of the place" must be defended from the encroachment of the metropolitan error of mistaking expense for "real" taste. Viewed from the village, these inroads are all "false ornaments" and can only be resisted by "contemplating nature herself in a simple, unbroken form." A "natural" wholeness is the model for composing a garden. The literary correlative is the epic poem whose plan is "great, entire, and one." Only things genuine and in place are allowed. "Nothing of foreign conceits which bad poets, or bad gardeners are always ready to introduce."

Humphrey Repton joined the battle of political analogies in his attack included in the 1796 edition of Price's *Essay*. He turned the tables on Price by claiming the middle position in garden art and government for himself. Repton charged Price with "deducing gardening from the painter's study of wild nature, and deducing government from the uncontrolled opinions of man in a savage state." By casting Price in the role of an extreme partisan, Repton is able to claim as his own the happy medium where neatness and simplicity result from a balance between "the wildness of nature and the stiffness of art." In exactly the same analogy Price used, Repton characterized the English constitution as "the happy medium betwixt the liberty of savages, and the restraint of despotic government." But he closes his tactical ploy with a statement that clearly identifies him as a practitioner of exclusion by suggesting that the likes of Price make their experiments in "untried, theoretical improvement" in some other country.

Price's answer, not surprisingly, accepts Repton's characterization of the English constitution, but he goes right to the heart of Repton's last statement by warning that such exclusion would produce "tameness and monotony" through the suppression of "freedom, energy and variety." Price understands the circumstantial nature of the controversy; after all he has already said he would have argued for neatness and regularity had the dominant fashion been for the roughness and irregularity of the Picturesque. And because of his more complex grasp of the argument, he is able to point out that the progress from oppression to anarchy "is not more natural, than from the ease of freedom and security, to indolence and apathy." He takes the opportunity to sound a warning that goes beyond the immediate conditions so compelling to everyone: "Let England beware; let her guard no less against the one, than against the other extreme; they generate each other in succession, for apathy invites oppression, and oppression is the parent of anarchy."

When Payne Knight discusses the importance of the sensory stimuli, even when he immediately organizes them according to the operations of the mind, he is attacked for focusing undue attention on its baser operations. Any appeal to initial stages of human behavior is an affront to those who place blind faith in the present stage of human society and its proprieties. *The British Critic* took issue with Knight's "rash impiety of the French school," for "the degrading system which claims kindred with the monkey . . . and attempts to derive all the powers of man from a few merely animal instincts." By talking about the initial operations of the mind in terms of pleasure and pain, Knight is seen as overturning all the accumulated wisdom of civilization. *The British Critic*, a notably conservative journal that tolerated little sympathy with revolutions or social experiments, reviewed the treatise "Principles of Political Association in a State" (1796) by Reverend John Brand, by noting that "different countries, in different ages of the world, have suffered very severe calamities from the operation of too extensive principles of liberty and equality."

George Mason worried about the conclusions that could be drawn from the libertarian effect of the Picturesque. "In this country the spirit of liberty extends itself to the very fancies of individuals. Independency has been as strongly asserted in matters of taste, as in religion and government; it has produced more motley appearances, than perhaps a whole series of ages can parallel. Yet to this whimsical exercise of caprice the modern improvements in gardening may chiefly be attributed." "Motley" compositions are clearly a threat. Individuals who abuse the enticements of liberty fall into the dreaded excess of license. They exercise their independence to no greater end than the pursuit of irresponsible personal whimsy. As we have noted before, one way to turn away the threat of the Picturesque was to demean it with a charge of frivolity. What is motley to some is restorative mixture to others.

It comes as no surprise that, if traditional Whigs attacked the Picturesque and its association with liberal doctrines, conservative Tories thought even less of the unholy alliance. Knight's alignment with Charles James Fox may have been what cost him membership in the Literary Club in 1785. It had also cost him his seat in Parliamant in the disastrous election of 1784. Knight did not have to leave the House, however. He was returned by the constituency immediately to the east, in Ludlow.

Although religious liberty was not a leading issue in these discussions of political liberty, it occasionally entered into the commentary. Intolerant religious systems which allowed no salvation except their own, whether based in modern Rome or in Scotland, were compared to despotic landscape improvement. "Knox and Brown differ very little in their manner of proceeding; no remnant of old superstition, or old taste, however rich and venerable, was suffered to remain, and our churches and gardens have been equally stripped of their ornaments." Price, seizing another opportunity to support his leading principle of mixture, cites the citizens of ancient Rome for their toleration of every style of worship, mixed and incorporated with their own. Voltaire had already observed that "a single religion in a country spelt tyranny, and two a civil war, but a multitude meant peace."

Payne Knight's own political actions in his neighborhood clearly indicate a man with little tolerance for disturbances. In 1819 as a local magistrate he organized a cavalry charge against colliers, but at the same time he was not in favor of enlarging the army to deal with civil emergencies. The latter position upheld the Whig principle of keeping power from centralizing around the king. Local matters could be dealt with in local ways.

Knight's fear of "popular commotion" expressed in 1795 was based on the appearance of an unmixed population of the laboring poor concentrated in the manufacturing towns. Whenever a large body, political or visual, presented an even, level, or systematic face, the Whig and the theorist of the Picturesque immediately became wary. The result of popular commotion could be to "re-plunge Europe into Barbarism." Barbarism was not a condition of salvation, a return to nature. It represented a loss of distinctions whether social, cultural, or economic. Power in the barbaric state was direct, unmixed, and therefore brutal. By introducing abrupt variation, the Picturesque attacked all systems that encouraged sameness or levelness. Anything that tended to reduce distinctions with some blended composition, of course, attracted its attention. "To level, in a very usual sense of the word, means to take away all distinctions, a principle that, when made general, and brought into action by any determined improver, either of grounds or govern-ments, occasions such mischiefs as time slowly, if ever, repairs, and which are hardly more dreaded by monarchs than painters." Level-ing had a bad name stemming from the dissenters and Puritans of the previous century whose attacks on monarchs were painful mem-ories. The Picturesque does not side with radicals any more than it sides with despots.

While Edmund Burke argued for the organic relationships in a society, cultivated over many years, where every connection be-tween people was direct and immediate, he was arguing against the indirect, abstract relationships posited by the radicals in England in sympathy with the French Revolution. The alignment that could be made between these abstract ideals and the effects of "the market" set impersonal workings against the operations of a culture that embodied the spirit of a people.

Two years after Knight published his poem, *The Landscape*, he published *Progress of a Civil Society*. It celebrated "respect for private rights," as the best support for public good. The unequal distribution of property assured the triumph of liberty over license. If a unitary power were to rule, its leveling effect would require the suppression of individual feelings of opposition. The result: "every passion, as 'tis more confined, / More fiercely rages in the narrow mind." The effect of long-term confinement is not healthy either to the one confined or to the power that is exercising the confinement. Letting off the pressure in irregular increments saves violent revolution. The relief cannot be predictable lest it become a reminder of the bonds. And it cannot be allowed to occur all at once because all patterns of distinction and connection would be destroyed in the deluge.

In the clearest statement of the complexity of liberty in the political realm, Knight pleads:

> O, may the useful folly still endure,
> Nor ask from reason a fallacious cure!
> Still may we value its unreal prize,
> Nor learn of silly sophists to be wise!
> For still delusion must support the plan
> Of social union, which it first began;—
> If abstract reason only rules the mind,
> In sordid selfishness it lives confined;
> And feels no other interest than its own.

Such an argument is an easy target for those who think they know patronizing when they see it. It suggests that power confers clear purpose and the absence of power instills gullibility. The folly is "useful" because it excludes those who do not know a plan is being perpetrated. The possibility that delusion envelops everyone does not seem to have occurred to Knight.

The crossover between landscape and political metaphor occurs with regularity in Knight's poem *Civil Society*. Liberty allows individual flowering, while tyranny holds all in check. Natural growth, free and unconstrained, is the best way for both tree and man to live. Should the aspirations of a tree's top or a man's hope be subjected to rigid repression, unfruitful shoots and mean vices appear at the base. "Reason itself becomes a useless tool, / When bent by force, and modified by rule; / And every flower of fancy blasted dies, / When tyrant laws direct it where to rise." For Knight, as well as other well-satisfied Englishmen of the period, Britain had managed to combine "order and rule with liberty."

The dynamic balance that the writers on the Picturesque sought was a classical way to compose contending forces. The toleration of somewhat more license than had usually been acceptable generally distinguishes their commentaries from more conservative ideals. But William Mason in his poem *The English Garden* saw the balance between reason and instinct threatened. Both of them seemed loosened from their proper places; they had become wayward as they veered from their respective pole. The resulting instability troubled Mason as he remembered a "golden time / When each created being kept of sphere / Appointed, nor infring'd its neighbor's right."

The crossover from political subject to landscape metaphor happens with a regularity comparable to the use of political metaphor in discussions of landscape design. William Mason likens each plant in a garden to "the people of a free-born state, / Its rights fair franchised." Liberty for plants is found in the enjoyment of air, showers, and sunshine.

Liberty stands as a prerequisite for the Picturesque to operate. Constraint either in its making or in its perception closes down the free play of discovery that engenders the Picturesque. In order for a patterned sensory experience to reach full effect in a viewer, the mind must be free to take it in. Only when the "imagination was at liberty" would it produce its "fullest perfection." Archibald Alison's *Essays on the Nature and Principles of Taste* (1790) furthers the associationist analysis with its emphasis on the conditions in the perceiving mind at the time of an aesthetic experience. A man in pain or in grief will not feel admiration for a scene or a form that would otherwise bring him delight. The effects of such scenes or forms are "most favorable when the imagination is free and unembarrassed." The ideal occurs when the attention is "so little occupied by any private or particular object of thought, as to leave us open to all the impressions, which the objects that are before us can produce. It is upon the vacant and the unemployed, accordingly, that the objects of taste make the strongest impression." Such an observation, of course, is a striking social statement. Being at ease, free from the strain of metabolic survival, is a prerequisite to the entire compositional ideal under review here. Whether there are degrees of ease or short durations of vacating the everyday struggle is another matter.

The Picturesque was considered by Humphrey Repton among others as a more accessible aesthetic mode than more traditional and respectable ones. It required less training and education than classical canons, and less fortitude than the Sublime. Its mildness produced charms for "common observers." By its nature, it was inclusive. The distinctions necessary to produce compositions for either the Beautiful or the Sublime could not be so sharply drawn when considering a picturesque composition. For this reason a greater range of people could participate with less preparation. It seemed open and accessible to common sense.

Price produced the clearest alignment of the principles of landscape design with political structure when he wrote:

"A good landscape is that in which all the parts are free and unconstrained, but in which, though some are prominent, and highly illuminated, and others in shade and retirement—some rough, and others more smooth and polished, yet they are all necessary to the beauty, energy, effect, and harmony of the whole. I do not see how a good government can be more exactly defined; and as this definition suits every style of landscape, from the plainest and simplest to the most splendid and complicated, and excludes nothing but tameness and confusion, so it equally suits all free governments, and only excludes anarchy and despotism. It must be always remembered, however, that despotism is the most complete leveller; and he who clears and levels every thing round his own lofty mansion, seems to me to have very Turkish principles of improvement."

Advocates of the Picturesque presented a complex, but consistent argument for compositions that, in effect, continuously renegotiated their status. They pushed forward to freedom and pulled back from license. Their ingenuity may have failed them as they explored the new compositional possibilities presented by the Picturesque. But their continuous engagement with political implications clearly shows how inclusive was their intention.

another issue for the modern— who includes + who excludes

ARTIFICE

T

he Picturesque is a mode of composition that stands next to nature, but does not imagine it is natural. By choosing to represent nature, to make an artifact that employs natural elements or the appearance of natural forces, it does not convey nature directly. As a result it was attacked for trifling with nature, for masquerading in nature's motley cloak, when it would have been more honest either to present clearly its artifice or to step aside deferentially and let nature stand free. The paradox is inescapable when Uvedale Price describes the Picturesque as not imitating, but "directing" accidents, "which are commonly called *nature*, in opposition to what is called *art*." His sensitivity to the paradox is expressed in his defense that he "did not argue for wildness only." If that were the case, then he would be no different from those who looked to nature for direct inspiration. The charge of "improving by neglect and accident" ignores the picturesque compositional ideal that seeks to follow the nature in Tasso's *Jerusalem Delivered* who "playfully imitates her imitators."

Unlike the Sublime or even the Beautiful, the Picturesque straightaway engages in representation. To those earnestly searching for a natural origin for their aesthetics, or their politics, the Picturesque was unreliably artificial. It would not settle down to the illusion of searching for a stable identity. By appearing to underplay control, the Picturesque severs any obvious connection between means and ends. Withholding resources throws all conclusions about appearances into question and it is this move that seems artificial when compared to a straight-through expenditure of effort that seems "natural."

Deception lies at the heart of the Picturesque, or so its detractors would have it. Anytime the clear display of compositional
control is avoided, they assume something suspicious is going on.
Interrupting the direct expression of available resources can be seen
as a sinister ploy to put one off guard. In a similar situation, the
detractors would not hold back, if for no other reason than to
display their pride. In no way would they miss the opportunity to
show their new acquisition to the fullest.

Another reason for distrusting apparent deception is a belief
in the redemptive potential of power clearly exercised. The Picturesque has a completely different meaning if one has already become
familiar with the exercise of control. Inducing the thrill of taking
risks by underutilizing power can produce a particular kind of
aesthetic resonance. Early, more undeveloped stages in the evolution of culture and technology, as well as lower economic levels
within a given society, provide artifacts that delight more powerful
visitors in search of a restorative glance at simplicity. Viewed from
a comfortable cushion of well-being, more primitive peoples seem
to live a life of direct expression and natural continuity. Touring
with roughness is yet another way to describe the Picturesque

By engaging in artifice, the Picturesque had to deal carefully
with the artificial. If nature means species of plants in their "natural"
habitat, then clearly exotic specimens brought back from a colonial
empire to its island home in the North Atlantic disregarded natural
and domestic virtues. William Mason gleefully reported on the
retribution that nature imposed when it sent down "The pelting
storm with icy bullets," to break the fragile barrier of the glassy
greenhouse. Foreign plants shiver when unprotected and eventually
fade and die when only human artifice tries to protect them.

The Picturesque alternative shifted between nature and artifice. In 1759, Edward Young's book *Conjectures on Original Composition*
argued that: "An Original may be said to be of a vegetable nature;
it rises spontaneously from the vital roots of genius; it grows, it is
not made. Imitations are often a sort of manufacture, wrought up by

those mechanics, art and labour, out of pre-existent materials, not their own." For Young original composition soared in the "regions of liberty"; they did not "move in the soft fetters of easy imitation."

For Knight and Price, liberty was found in not making such an absolute choice: either nature or art. The Picturesque used nature to make its own compositions. Origin was not the point. Things that grew could be combined with things that were arranged. Obedience to organic nature was no less tyranny than submission to a political despot. Man's imagination and inventions were no less powerful expressions of liberty than nature's raw forms. After all, Alexander Pope had recommended consultation with the genius of the place, not capitulation.

Most who supported or attacked the Picturesque fell victim to the more-natural-than-thou temptation. Nature remained the model for Mason, for example, who felt it needed some trimming. The contrasts of visual stimuli are not simply categorical possibilities invented by man; they are imitations of nature's own patterns. His genius of the place is a sylvan despot who is "patient and placable." Those who do him loyal service and revere his dignity, rather than rebel against him, are rewarded when he easily blends their effort with his own. The poet's task, whether working with words or landscape, is only to "frame the fence," to set the limits of the compositions, not to rearrange or reconstitute the raw materials. Mason attacked the skepticism he found in the opening lines of Knight's *Progress of a Civil Society*. The abstract consideration of the origins of human society seemed a dangerous folly that stepped outside the conventions given by history and religion and engaged in a free play of possibilities.

Not only does the Picturesque play fast and loose with sacred nature when it should be obedient to it, it also distorts common-sense demands for comfort and utility. The conflict between art and comfort appears clearly in *A Picturesque Guide to Bath*, whose author no sooner leaves London than he encounters a decaying wooden bridge at Datchet that is about to be replaced by a stone one. This change stimulates consideration of the relative claims of art and convenience. "It is to be regretted, that what is most conducive to comfort is not always the most pleasing to the eye." On the simplest visual level, a structure whose decrepitude has produced various departures from strict regularity is to be replaced by one that will be firmly in place and accurately aligned with structurally stable intentions.

A certain delight will be missing in the new bridge. The eye enjoys departures from the regularity that the mind uses to keep track of things. The mind attends to objects for their abstracted, representative value, rather than for their immediate sensory stimuli. The irregular form, color, and outline of a decaying bridge draw our sensory attention. But further, the mind also takes delight in reflecting on an object whose very weakness separates it from the bustle of means and ends. The new stone bridge will no doubt fulfill the expectations of firmness for use as well as completion of form. In so doing it will settle back into a visual field attended to with a very different aesthetic expectation. Its newness and initial novelty will draw attention as well, but the expression of pride and strength will be a significant proportion of the delight it produces. As the description goes on: the "artist will behold the exchange with a sigh; and while he acknowledges the deference due to public convenience, will still, in his own mind, and for his own purposes prefer the present tottering structure." The sigh is itself characteristic of an attitude that considers improvement a reminder of how the expression of power calls out for an antidote. The Picturesque is such a reminder. It keeps insisting on mixture through inclusion of the marginal condition. In the face of the power exerted to construct the stone bridge, the attention that the Picturesque pays to the decaying condition of the wooden one seems artificial to those committed to progress. The "natural" evolution of progress, a notion that gained considerable force during the time of technological advances at the turn of the nineteenth century, seems to overwhelm these artful sighs with a mechanical cacophony.

The Picturesque fiddled with nature, mixing it with extraneous matters, and its practice tended to remove functioning parts of the human landscape from their natural place to set them aside for aesthetic contemplation even as it intensified the natural appearance. To remove land for ornamental gardens was one thing; to make land look like a potential source of game or wood or water and then not to make use of it except for visual stimulus was at the very least extravagant if not perverse. When the land is the primary source of the means for human survival, such enclosure is socially irresponsible. We need only remember the curious status of Tityrus's protected farm in Virgil's First Eclogue to grasp the significance of this charge.

When Knight recommends that "trees and creepers, . . . ought to be as little disturbed, as is consistent with comfort," he describes a thin line separating commonsense comfort from the distortion introduced by unnatural aesthetic principles. Even if "the character of nature is more pleasing than any that can be given by art," wild growth assaulting a human refuge is a little too close to a nightmare of barbarism. Price's realism admits that "near the house picturesque beauty must, in many cases, be sacrificed to neatness," because he identifies picturesque beauty with an unimproved state. That state is "frequently, and irrevocably destroyed" by committed improvers largely because it represents a slow, marginal accumulation patiently awaiting human purposes. Once it is disturbed, it is difficult to recreate in a synthetic, accelerated way.

When Richard Payne Knight built Downton Castle with its irregular outline and classical interiors, he also made alterations in the valley of the Teme River to enhance its quality as a picture. Primarily this consisted of removing any sign of productive activity. Beauty is ascribed to objects or scenes when they are wrenched from their place in a continuous flow of productivity or when they fall out of place by age or desuetude. In 1817, Knight removed iron forges and a furnace that were remnants of the source of his family's wealth. He converted a canal serving the factory into a pool fed by the river to supply a small, but very beautiful, waterfall. Later he converted the site of a forge into cottage gardens. The Picturesque attaches itself to times and places whose subsided energy permits consumption in an underplayed manner.

One of the most powerful attacks on the Picturesque from the pragmatic and commonsense point of view was launched by William Marshall, styled as a practitioner and writer on landscape gardening, in his review of *Landscape* and *Essay on the Picturesque* (1795). His political orientation is evident from his inclusion, by permission, of the gardening portion of Horace Walpole's "Anecdotes on Painting" in his earlier publication *Planting and Ornamental Gardening: A Practical Treatise* (1785). His sharp perception quickly picks up the political style of the Picturesque as a "bush-fighting mode of attack." His acid pen ridicules both Price and Knight by pushing their arguments to the extreme. He rejects any speculation that carries "rural ornament" away from the way things really are, out there in the land. Painting is no help largely because the landscape is viewed by a moving perceiver and any commentary on the land that is "all libraries and picture galleries" can only be misleading. Marshall accepts that painting employs "ingenious deceptions," but the land is too serious and fundamental to be anything but "the open display of facts."

His interest in having the dominant composition of the land be seen as an irreducible fact, so as to blunt questions how it operates and how it came to be the way it is, establishes itself by appealing to commonsense experience that seems to give stature to ordinary people. By locating the attack on the Picturesque in individual experience, he flatters its importance as he deflects the potential for those same individuals to question the ownership and control of the land. Marshall's withering response to Price and Knight is surely stimulated by his instant realization how threatening are their appeals to consider recomposing nature and artifice.

The Picturesque is not functional according to Marshall. By seeking to lay siege to an inhabited house by unwholesome swamps

full of creeping, crawling gnats, toads, and water rats, the Picturesque rightly reduces it to an experience one would prefer to view
rather than live in. Wild scenery is best brought indoors as "furniture." Price and Knight's recommendations inevitably lead to living
in huts, wearing sheepskins, and going unwashed and uncombed,
according to Marshall. "The conveniences of life must give place to
the Picturesque."

Marshall's hardheaded realism is salutary, even if it is ultimately employed for nefarious ends. He recognizes that descriptions of
how one responds to a landscape scene depend on the state of mind
of the viewer. "Any one who has had repeated occasion to view,
with critical regard, the same scene, under the self-same circumstances, . . . must have experienced emotions extremely various, if
not, in some degree at least, contradictory." While a painting's fixed
quietness may stimulate a desire for increased irritation and intricacy, a real landscape is replete with constant changes in sound,
light, intervention of tree branches, movement of animals and
birds, and smells.

Rather than being the sign of despotism, Marshall finds turn-
ing public footpaths away from a house or the removal of cottages
done simply "to obtain the security and the domestic comforts
attached to a suitable degree of retirement." Those who judge
everything from the point of view of painting can happily live in
their unreal world where all people are "excellent moral characters"
who "have no faculty of finding things before they are lost, no wish
to rob hen roosts, nor to assist servants to rob their masters." He
calls Price to task by reminding him that his uncle, while not an
aristocrat, but a well-disposed country squire, only visited his lesser
neighbors, and that although he communicated freely with the
yeomanry on rural information and improvements, did "not live in
the same village with them."

Both landscape painting and pastoral poetry present a train of
fanciful ideas for those "who have never seen a flock of sheep, nor
have had occasion to observe the stupid insensibility of shepherds

and shepherdesses." The Picturesque, by "forever labouring to strike out unthought-of agreements and contrasts," is forever "suspicious and suspected." Its "whole aim is deception." Given the possibilities that can present themselves when new compositions are considered, it is no wonder that William Marshall wishes to stamp out this dangerous contagion that makes deception an activity free and open instead of opaque and defensive.

A conflict perceived between the Picturesque and the useful reinforces the estimation of some commentators that the Picturesque was dangerously artificial. Its passivity in the face of nature's untended accumulation is vulnerable to the progress of agriculture. The Picturesque relies on the marginal usages of places and people. When "wild thickets are converted into scenes of plenty and industry, and when gypsies and vagrants give way to . . . husbandmen, and their attendants," the Picturesque is diminished. In a departure from an earlier estimation of the nobility required for decay, Price boldly proposes that "not just grand ruins, but old mills" can contribute to picturesque scenes. The derelict condition of formerly productive structures is a pleasing feature not only of ancient implements, but contemporary ones as well. The transforming vision of the Picturesque can incorporate almost anything, once its drops out of the productive race.

One of the central charges against the Picturesque is that it conceals hard facts, that it lulls the powerful into an illusion of ease and patronizes those who have yet to enjoy the rewards of sophisticated rusticity. There is ample evidence in the eighteenth-century commentaries on the Picturesque to support that charge. William Mason, not one to probe too closely into the complexities of the aesthetic mode, recommends that trees be placed "to mask some broad roof / Perchance of glaring tile that guard the stores / Of Ceres; or the patched disjointed choir / Of some Fame." Trees can also be used "To veil what e're of wall, or fence uncouth / Disgusts the eye, which tyrant use has reared, / And stern Necessity forbids to change." Knight counters by saying that, in contrast to "current practice that hides 'offices' of a country house making it wretched, solitary and square," he accepts the variety of all sorts of necessary intrusions. "With reference to Mr. Repton: I choose to retain, what offends him so much, cross roads and directing posts within 200 yards of my house, rather than sacrifice, as he has done in so many instances, all the charms of retirement, intricacy, and variety to the vanity of splendid approach, or the ostentasion of undivided property. "

For an example of what Price calls "the naked, solitary appearance of a house" whose offices are totally concealed underground, we need only refer to William Chambers's Marino Casino (1767–71), originally published in the 1739 *Treatise on Civil Architecture*, that reappeared as an end pavilion at Harewood House. The kitchen and scullery in the basement are sunk below ground level in a dry moat. Only the pavilion is visible on the landscape.

The economic resources of the Picturesque are plentiful; it is not the aesthetic style of people who are ragged by necessity. But it aims at a delight that is protected from direct economic activity. It is an escape from getting and spending. Its status as a vacation from stern necessity can elicit outrage from those at work in the scene. "Self-improvement, crowned with self-content," is a satisfactory image for this self-induced illusion.

Nostalgia seems inevitably linked with the Picturesque. In the relaxed drift of nostalgia one turns aside from the oncoming rush of present events. Images elicited by nostalgia were once part of that rush, but their impact has been deflected by time and memory. The plenitude on which the Picturesque relies exists in the accumulation of the past, both in the mind and on the ground. Nostalgia is power deferred. It does not ask that someone take responsibility for it. It is a picture. Picturesque colors are not the fresh, delicate ones of spring, but those of autumn whose age and decay bespeak fulness and repose tinged with memory and the sharpness of abrupt terminations.

The accumulation that underlies and precedes the exercise of the Picturesque is made quite clear by Uvedale Price when he sets up the most "pleasant" situation for improvement by "opening gradually a scene, where the materials are only too abundant." A woods, "left to itself, and not a bough cut for twenty or thirty, or any number of years" is the perfect opportunity "to give variety to this rich but uniform mass" by partial clearing. "In forests and in old parks, the rough bushes nurse up young trees and grow up with them; and thence arises that infinite variety of openings, of inlets, of glades, of forms of trees, &c. The effect of all these might be preserved, and rendered more beautiful, by a judicious style and degree of clearing and polishing, and might be successfully imitated in other parts." Apparently neglect can produce either a uniform mass or infinite variety. One case suggests intervention, the other imitation. Nature, therefore, is not a constant model. Sometimes its appearance is acceptable, but other times, human artifice must be mixed in to meet the compositional requirements of the Picturesque.

The suggestion of passivity introduced by nostalgia and preservation is reinforced when Price takes issue with his memory of Crabbe's poem "The Library," in which the poet personified Neglect as active. For the production of picturesque effects, Price prefers of think of Neglect as possessing inertia, even as it remains a powerful agent. Of course it is not merely passive. The Picturesque results from a rhythm of judicious trimming and cultivated neglect. Maintenance is accomplished, not by obsessive interventions every day to realign the materials according to an obvious pattern of control, but rather to let neglect proceed, watch for the interaction of its characteristic patterns with human intentions on both large and small scales, and then to intervene at irregular stages.

When the Picturesque was named for landscape compositions that looked like pictures, it was more than merely noticing a superficial likeness. Pictures carried a different kind of truth than words. Because the representation produced by words is not made of the same stimuli as the scene they purport to re-present, something is lost in the translation. Pictures, however, operated on the same sensory receptors, seemingly without serious intervention. As the commentator on the picturesque views of Bath asserted: It is more the business of the pencil to impress correct ideas on the mind than of the tongue or pen. "It is to forms we have recourse, when words are inadequate to the conveying our conceptions." But immediately having said this, the commentator acknowledges that the artist's pencil can produce either a "composition" or a "portrait." Correcting deformities and discord is something that an artist does and the resulting composition is hardly a neutral conveyance of natural truth.

The proposal, identified by its very name, that the Picturesque makes with regard to landscape design is that to arrange compositions of natural objects one must consult pictures. To most hostile commentators, this recommendation seemed the height of folly, a totally unnecessary step. If one wishes to arrange gardens, go look at nature directly, not stay indoors looking at paintings, or even worse, reading books. Study is unnecessary; immediate experience with real nature is all that is required. For the Picturesque, of course, studying paintings and books was the clearest recognition that designing the landscape was a complex amalgam of raw sensory patterns supplied by nature with the patterns of arrangement and selection inherent in the operation of the human mind. There are "reasons for studying copies of nature, though the original is before us." The resulting landscape compositions were the just combination of two natures, God's and man's.

basis for the modern—

By recognizing the value of "copies," the Picturesque is stepping aside from the vain pursuit of the "original" as the only way to begin a composition. Nature does not function for the Picturesque the way it does for those who wish to use it as an unimpeachable justification. This single move by the advocates of the Picturesque probably irritated their opponents more than any other. Natural rights, natural landscapes all appeal to some ultimate source for their power. The Picturesque does not. It admits, not freely, but with great trepidation, that "separating, selecting and combining" is what we do, and must take responsibility for doing.

Why and how one should consult pictures, or literature for that matter, in preparation for making a landscape composition occupied Price and Knight and others who tried to avoid a naturist illusion. Knight recognized the separate contributions of the stimulated retina and the perceiving mind. The painter, in order to make a picture, must be able to separate these components. The "appearance" of an object must be registered as a two-dimensional pattern for it to be deposited on the surface for drawing or painting. "Painting, as it imitates only the visible qualities of bodies, separates those qualities from all others, even those that in reality are offensive to other senses or understanding." This "natural" seeing, meaning with a minimum of accumulated association, is attained only through special training. The trained painter must capture the image that strikes the retina as a pattern. Copying what the mind knows to be true from the concurrent testimony of other senses and from the associations of memory is not representing what the eye sees. The act of cutting off the mind's contributions in the interest of isolating the retina's image is not a "natural" one, however. It is the self-conscious artifice required to make a picture that will look like a picture. Whether the casual viewer must go through the same training in order to see "naturally" is a question that repeatedly vexed apologists of the Picturesque. They knew that this crucial step must be taken to make a picture. They were intrigued by the paradox of having to take an artificial step away from common experience in order to meet common expectations about the value of pictures.

The newly won status of landscape painting and the fascination with optics and perspective introduce other mechanisms that make the relation between paintings, nature, and viewer a complex matter. Imitation, subjectivity, and convention could compromise any set of relations that strived to "get it right." Because the Picturesque avoided such a pitfall, it opened up, if it did not pursue every possibility, a reflexive process that can be carried forward even now.

The creator of Painshill garden southwest of London, Charles Hamilton, "not only had studied pictures, but had studied them for the express purpose of improving real landscape. The place he created (a task of quite another difficulty from correcting, or adding to natural scenery) fully proves the use of such a study." Price found the pleasing quality of this rescue operation of a most unpromising hillside along the River Mole to be, "not from what *had*, but from what had *not* been done; it had no edges, no borders, no distinct lines of separation; nothing was done, except keeping the ground properly neat, and the communication free from any obstruction. The eye and the footsteps were equally unconfined; and if it is a high commendation to a writer or a painter, that he knows when to leave off, it is not less so to an improver." The sensitivity the Picturesque advocates felt for underplaying, rather than overplaying, is appealed to once again.

In an attempt to convince people that consultations beyond original nature were advantageous, Price asserted that "The language (if it may be so called) by which objects of sight make themselves intelligible, is exactly like that of speech." The linguistic analogy could not be more clearly drawn. He went on to compare the advantages gained in reading literature for the living of life. The reader of literature is not only responding to isolated characters in the story, but to the structure of relations and "the effect on each other." "This appears to me a true and exact statement of the mutual relation that painting and nature bear to each other." Subsequent experiences in one's life are given a wider set of references that are recalled, in part, because they are shaped and memorable. Paintings as well are more memorable, and therefore more useful, because their compositions are "the only *fixed* and *unchanging* selections from the works of nature." The mixture of the immediate changes in the natural world with the fixed patterns of human constructions enriches present experience by reference to something not present. Price summed up the complex relation between pictures and nature by suggesting that they "throw a reciprocal light" on each other. In the picturesque mode one is not privileged over the other; they affect each other. Nature is different because of painting; painting is different because of nature.

William Mason's *English Garden* expresses the general fascination of trying to incorporate the lesson of painting into landscape design. His translation of Fresnoy's *Art of Painting* prepares him to "call on the Muse of painting to instruct" the gardener. The conventions of "three marked distances" and "Fancy's apt concealments" are the most immediate effect that painting had on landscape design. In the preface to the poem he demonstrates the easy crossover between the arts that supports his whole argument and finds artifice the natural consequence of artistic activity. "Art at the same time, in rural improvements, pervading the province of Nature, unseen and unfelt, seemed to bear a striking analogy to that species of verse, the harmony of which results from measured quantity and varied cadence, without the too studied arrangement of final syllables, or regular return of consonant sounds." But Mason employs the analogy with nature because he firmly believes that its genuineness supports the artifice.

Moving from one artistic medium to another is a sure sign to skeptics that the virtues of each are being compromised. Exchange, trade, and transference are the mechanisms that inexorably move away from original meanings. Of course a poem about a garden is full of transferences. William Mason opens Book Three of his poem with traditional statements about the power of language: "that force of antient phrase which, speaking, paints, and is the thing it sings." The writers on the Picturesque practiced borrowing metaphors from all sorts of sources. The commentary that William Burgh added to the 1783 edition of Mason's poem includes gardening as a liberal art along with poetry and painting. Exchanges between sister arts is scarcely trading with heathens.

When commonsense perception is called base or backward and sophisticated minds recommend taking up an artificial posture, guardians of public morality are quick to issue warnings of impending decline. From its advocacy of mixing ordinary experience with extremes of sophisticated artifice, the Picturesque attracted critics who wrapped themselves in the camouflage of nature. When the Picturesque asserts the need for compositional relationships and at the same time emphasizes the energy of the sensory stimuli, its complex position opens it to charges of being either so confused that any straight-thinking person should reject it out of hand or so devious that any right thinking person will stay away from it. The *Critical Review* of November 1805 chose to ridicule the Picturesque for directing attention to the "mere organic sensation" by saying "to talk of a taste for mere light, shade, and color is surely an absurdity confusing taste and feeling."

The gardener Humphrey Repton was perpetually offended by Price and Knight's artificial response to the land. As men who wrote more than they dug, they were fatally separated, Repton believed, from any connection with the origins of the landscape. Their arrogation of "good taste" to their own sophisticated ways rankled him. He responded by embracing a conscientious concern for humanity by saying: "In whatever relates to man, propriety and convenience are not less objects of good taste than picturesque effect." He went on to suggest that Price and Knight's habitual contact with paintings and "bold and picturesque scenery" may have rendered them "insensible to the beauty of those milder scenes that have charms for common observers." "I will not arraign your taste, or call it vitiated, but your palate certainly requires a degree of 'irritation' rarely to be expected in garden scenery." Not only is nature a reliable guide, but human nature is worthy of decent respect according to Repton. From both sides, the Picturesque seemed unnecessarily exclusive and artificial. Both Repton and Gilpin shared a straightforward, commonsensical approach to the landscape. They avoided speculation on the complexities that might underlie their pleasure in looking at picturesque scenes. Gilpin described and sketched; Repton dug and planted.

A sophisticated designer setting out to create a rustic appearance risked making something that looked contrived. To label a design "contrived" is to point out a gap between a relaxed intention and the obvious strain introduced to achieve it. If the effort required to create and maintain a landscape composition is not obvious, contrivance is not an issue. Knight was against contrived rusticity because it did not convince. The Picturesque worked when the artifice successfully posed a question about its status. To make its presence unmistakable or completely concealed is to leave out the primary experience of actively probing and questioning what one sees. Successful artifice meant completely different things to its producer and to those who were to be convinced by it. It is difficult sometimes to be certain for whom controversy over the Picturesque was pursued.

One of the problems for any new garden composition is its newness. Small plants, freshly shaped slopes look, for a time at least, raw and obvious. Price was offended by such scenes not only for their visual harshness, but for the system of production that was increasingly evident in England. "I have seen places on which large sums had been lavished, united so little with the landscape around them, that they gave me the idea of having been made by contract in London, and then sent down in pieces, and put together on the spot." The threat of remote, systematic production riding over local details surfaced in landscape design as well as economics. The intrusion, full of contrivance and artifice, stuck out from the existing continuity. That kind of abrupt variation is not the kind that pleased devotees of the Picturesque. Such scenes were "plainly artificial" and had the appearance of "having been made by a receipt." If there is plain artificial, there must be a concealed artificial that is more acceptable in some way. Artifice must be managed to make its presence uncertain. Making anything by recipe in an

automatic, unthinking way is to behave in accordance with a system
that does not take into consideration anything beyond itself.

Obvious artifice is preferred by anyone who wants to attract
attention by their skill or their expenditure. Architects and landscape designers were pleased to have their work noticed as evidence
of the demand for their services. Clients were pleased to have the
extent of their resources displayed for all to see. Each gained social
prominence by obvious activity, not by concealment and uncertainty whether anything had actually been done. Price roundly censur-
ed such "desire for celebrity by exciting the curiosity and admiration of the vulgar."

The artifice of shaping a composition in response to, or in
anticipation of, the audience, in other words the rhetorical stance,
seemed inappropriate when nature was the subject. But the advocates of the Picturesque knew that even nature as a concept is a
rhetorical creation and that compositional devices and metaphors
were the only way to address a present that was so far from the
innocent beginning in the Garden of Eden. Knight, in his opening
lines to the *Progress of a Civil Society*, describes the didactic or
philosophical poet as being unable to excite sympathies with his
reader. All he has to work with to "charm the sense" are the sensory
stimuli of rich and harmonious color. The other route into the
reader's attention is through the colder road of understanding based
on "the skill and correctness of drawing and composition."

Artifice suggests that what is seen is not the direct, trust-
worthy expression of an identifiable agent, but an artifact shaped
by anticipated responses. While "the spectator never knows when
he has seen all," the proprietor or contriver, indeed, knows all.
Artifice expresses a desire to hold back information about origin or
fabrication. As a consequence it can be seen as a deliberate misrepresentation of its intent. The appearance of casualness or spontaneity allows a response that accepts the expression with minimal
preparation. Seriousness or great effort are anticipated with some

preparation. Knight, echoing a long tradition including Castiglione, recommends that "propriety, perspicuity, elegance and simplicity . . . are obtained by labour and study, which must not only be employed, but concealed." Such a suggestion for matters of some importance is a familiar one in the history of art. But Knight is referring to "little or common things." Simplicity in little things seems a natural occurrence, not the subject of labor. For common things to obtain propriety and elegance seems an intrusion of smaller things on larger ones. This intrusion is, of course, at the heart of the pastoral in poetry and of the Picturesque.

To make a case for concealment is difficult. It almost always means that nefarious forces are at work. When Price tries to make that case, he continues the transference of examples from other arts to landscape design. "The improver should conceal himself like a judicious author, who sets his reader's imagination at work, while he seems not to be guiding, but exploring with him some new region. The improver employs his whole skill to lead the spectator in the best direction through the most interesting scenes, and towards the most striking points of view, and to facilitate his approach to them, he should not strive to confine him to one single route at all. There is in our nature a repugnance to despotism even in trifles, and we are never so heartily pleased as when we appear to have made every discovery ourselves." The appearance of being unguided and unconstrained seems to be the focus of the matter. Willing suspension of disbelief is one thing; not even knowing that something is being concealed is quite another. This problem is one more example of how the Picturesque depends on the accumulation of resources and knowledge to participate fully in the complexities of representation at work.

For William Mason, concealment is not a question, but an answer. He is not probing beyond the traditional view that art mends nature's features without changing them. This classical view of art's task was only tempered by the current taste for irregularity. Mason recommends broad contrast and variety. He censures dull uniformity, quaint contrivance, labored littleness, and mechanical order. These vices are the result of man's not picking up on nature's own careless graces, but insisting on an obvious exercise of rule.

He prefers patterns he finds in nature or that man makes by taking the path of least resistance, such as the hare's path, the milkmaid's step, or the path made by the plow.

Picturesque and pastoral concealment can certainly be a tactic of dominant power trying to obscure its operation in the interest of self-preservation. The threat of concealment is most acutely felt by an ideological position that believes only in clear abstractions. The similarity of this conclusion to the position of the radicals in England that supported the French Revolution is obvious. The defense of concealment usually takes the position of Edmund Burke when he attacked the upheaval across the Channel in "Reflections on the Revolution in France." Opposing clear abstractions, Burke took refuge in the tangle of historical developments in Britain to preserve the status quo. But Burke's defense is not the only one that can be made.

The Picturesque opposition to systematic power extends to economic domination as well. Price refers to the effect such power has on the landscape as "ravages of wealthy pride." Price was led to consider such intrusion by reading Goldsmith's poem "The Deserted Village." That story, "feelingly described," presents the lamentable impact that an absentee landlord has on the fictitious village of Auburn. An important distinction is being drawn between "wealthy pride" and "wealthy neglect." Price considers the former "no less hostile to real taste, than to humanity." Although this distinction seems to be putting him in league with Repton's concern for ordinary people, it is not so simple as that. Price finds refuge in a position that deflects the direct conflict between levels of control. He prefers incremental adjustments to be made continuously, knowing that a final resolution of conflict is as illusory as an ultimate origin found in nature. The desire for a resting place, either at a beginning or an end, may be understandable, but is not to be encouraged by acting as if it can be found.

Price also understands vanity. "Vanity is a general enemy to all improvement, and there is no such enemy to the real improvement of the beauty of grounds, as the foolish vanity of making a parade of their extent, . . . to appropriate by planting other clumps and patches of exotics which seem to stare about them, and wonder how they came there; to appropriate, by demolishing many a cheerful retired cottage, that interfered with nothing but the despotic love of exclusion (and make amends, perhaps, by building a village *regularly* picturesque)." "Adorning a real village, and promoting the comforts and enjoyments of its inhabitants" may be the only way that wealth can produce "natural and unaffected variety." Sameness and vacancy are all that solitary power can produce. The example that Price cites with evident disgust are the "sham towns and villages made to divert the Emperor of China; in which the various incidents of real life are acted by Eunuchs."

Although not part of the eighteenth-century commentaries under discussion, Japan provided some striking illustrations of spiritual and aesthetic plenitude avoiding the excesses of vanity. Within the climate of indigenous nature religion and Buddhist precepts of transiency, Japan has produced compositions that blend nature and artifice in ways that can be called Picturesque. The thirteenth-century poet Kamo-no Chomei wrote "Notes on a Ten-foot Square Hut" that traced his subsidence from vanity to humility as marked by describing a sequence of abodes. His last dwelling is no longer a solid, constructed thing, but a cocoon: natural, biodegradable, temporary. Its joints are not rigid, but hinged. Even his musical instrument, the koto, folds in half and his books of poetry and music lie in wait in leather baskets. The whole thing can be moved in two carts. "Only in a hut built for the moment can one live without fears." As this tiny abode settles on the ground, its intrusion, however light, causes the setting to adjust. A rock-lined pool fed by a bamboo pipe is added to bring delight to the transient inhabitant.

The available delights are free: seasonal sights, flowers, berries and nuts, trips to nearby sites mentioned by Heian poets. The views from the peak are owned by no one. And the peak itself is hardly awesome. His trips to the capital, for the stated purpose of begging, surely serve to remind him of his reasons for retiring at such a distance from the world. When he goes down to watch the river traffic, it suggests poetry, not labor.

His contact with other people is restricted to the family that lives on the mountain. He enjoys rambling about the countryside with the guardian of the mountain's son in whose company he is free of the fetters of social existence. The contact is comfortable because the boy's innocence and ignorance obscure the vast differences between them even as they share the same place on the mountain paths. He is the perfect companion to ratify Kamo's assumed rusticity. And someone else is responsible for the boy's survival. The contrast between the rustic family and this learned poet from the capital who plays music and goes to poetical sites is masked by the visual and spatial realms they share. The disparity is not evident until their interiors are revealed by speech or visits to their abodes. The posts and beams of the mountain guardian's hut do not have hinges, we can be sure. Transiency is a state of mind consciously posed against unreflective habitation. The poor man may live with it, but he does not entertain it, or cultivate it.

Kamo realizes that what he reserves for himself, the things that set him apart from the rustic setting, are impediments to his spiritual progress. Clothes of woven wisteria fiber may do very well, but their floral origin enfolds him in memories of purple radiance. His stated lack of ambition, posed against the bustle of the capital, is belied by the essay he is writing. His ambition is not of the moment, the immediate, but displaced into the future, into an absent realm. He continues to pare down the differences separating him from those who know little else but the mountain forests, but he cannot erase them. Of the disappointed poet on the next hill, who wrote nothing, and left even his lute and books behind, we, of course, know nothing. Kamo is not all that different from Goldsmith's son of Auburn trying vainly to get the right "look" of the tasteful absence of striving.

If landscape design is tangled in the lineaments of nature, architecture is much less so. When the Picturesque refers to buildings, artifice is much less of a problem. After all, it is precisely the linkage of artifice/house to nature/landscape that picturesque compositions are intended to forge, or weave, as the case may be. The idea of picturesque architecture is somewhat at odds with the traditional evolution of edifices that "refine and ennoble" the "porches of cottages and the rude posts that support them." Porticos and colonnades concentrate the desire for large-scale human artifacts that resist degradation by the effects of time or fashion. In so far as architecture makes singular, clear identities, it leaves behind "that quickly-changing variety and intricacy of form, and that correspondent light and shadow," constituting the distinct character of picturesque buildings.

Because picturesque buildings are a kind of throwback or reenactment of times or places that had less resources at their disposal, they are within "the power of men of moderate means." Architecture requires the large resources of "princes and those men with princely fortunes," but more lowly buildings can be improved by means of slight additions and alterations to produce picturesque compositions. It is precisely this apparent accessibility that leads to the end of complexity and the triumph of gross sensory abbreviation that characterizes the subsequent history of the Picturesque.

Attaching delight to Picturesque scenes often leads an author to make egregious attributions regarding the happiness of those who are to be found living in "naturally occurring" raggedness. William Mason blithely rhymes about "sweet simplicity" rolling over their happy heads. "They bask on sunny hillocks or desport in rustic pastime." This extension of visual delight felt by the powerful when viewing a picturesque scene to the denizens of the Picturesque surely deserves censure. To go further and assert that, therefore, all commentary on the Picturesque is tainted by such heartlessness seems unnecessary. But one cannot help but remember with some irritation Tityrus's lack of sympathy with his friend Meliboeus in Virgil's First Eclogue. The latter stanzas of Book Three of Mason's poem are particularly offensive in this regard.

In his poem *The Garden*, published in 1781, translated into English in 1789, and to which George Mason generously refers, Jacques de Lille expressed a fine sense of the complex arrangement of natural and constructed elements in garden design. "Nature and time and art and man combine / To bid rich accidents around us shine." Together these primary elements are arranged with "noble negligence." The apparent contradiction in that delicious phrase, seconded by Price's "wealthy neglect," are further explained when confusion and chance are the source of brightest beauty, but only when combined with "creative art." How one bids accidents to occur, how much chance remains when it is arranged by art are the questions that the Picturesque works with, but does not answer. The ideal of noble negligence is more understandable, if only as a cruel or delightful ruse. Negligence is not dangerous when there is no risk to one's status or position by momentarily letting things slide.

Whether artifice is a positive component in the Picturesque or a serious defect seems to depend on whether the presence of concealment, deception, and manipulation are considered benign or threatening. The use of these techniques has a greater chance of being judged positively if its operation is understood by all. Suspending disbelief is another form of power underutilized. One could choose to doubt, but does not do so in the interest of gaining something unattainable without belief. However, to perpetrate deception in the presence of those who do not know that they are subject to a misrepresentation is how power operates with direct

intent to minimize risk by using any devious technique it can employ. Artifice, even if it is dismissed as "mean and idle" by de Lille,
alternatively, as part of an actively argued convention, can extend
the depth of available resources by introducing or tolerating a
degree of turbulence in the relationship between the parallel con-
structs of nature and art.

CONNECTION

The picturesque conception of composition, in both its visual and political aspects, struggled to organize separate elements, whether they are aesthetic forms, or people, <u>without resorting to a "system</u>." The two fundamental means it used to mitigate the direct use of compositional power were mixture and the underutilization of that power. It was to be hoped that compositions resulting from these means would not fall into a system. The problem that remained was how to connect the parts so as to make something that might actually be recognizable as a composition. Both writers on the Picturesque, Uvedale Price and Richard Payne Knight, considered system to be antithetical to the ideal they were advocating. As a result they were always alert to any signs of systematic organization. "The fatal rock on which all professed improvers are likely to split, is that of system; they become mannerists, both from getting fond of what they have done before, and from the ease of repeating what they have so often practised." The habitual and the expected are opposed whether they appear in the career of landscape gardeners or in the visual patterns of the landscapes themselves. Newly finished places in the English countryside were suffering from an "eternal smoothness and sameness," according to Price.

Without the Picturesque, the design of landscape had become a "mechanical common-place operation" of relentless leveling, both in the improver's imagination and on the landscape itself. <u>The attachment to local settings and their power bases</u> is threatened by the growing impact of contracting "by the yard" as was common in the growing industrial districts around London. Systematic leveling

is this possible

stems from the repetition of mechanical processes as much as from professional or aesthetic habit. Smoothness is so easy that it re- quires "neither taste, nor invention, but merely the mechanical hand and eye of many a common labourer." Plodding mechanics must rely on rules to produce picturesque works valued only to the degree that they depart from the current system of smoothness. Artists of genius, by contrast, produce works that are necessarily "unequal and irregular; and produce much to blame and ridicule." There is a risk accepted by choosing to design in the Picturesque. Knight supports his censure of system by going back to the early discussions of this mode of composition and quoting Lord Shaftes- bury's "Advice to Authors": "The most ingenious way of becoming foolish is by a system."

If the Picturesque encourages the changefulness of novelty in the face of various systematic repetitions of control, it also tries to limit the scale of the parts that move: smaller than a whole "system," but larger than the smallest common denominator. According to William Gilpin, the picturesque eye was "to survey nature; not to anatomise matter. It throws its glance around in the broadest style. It comprehends an extensive tract at each sweep. It examines parts, but never descends to particles."

The Picturesque seeks to avoid a fracturing that will, for in- stance, undermine the significance of localized power, in landscape and political terms. The picturesque posture of contrast depends on a condition that has reached, is reaching, or might reach plenitude. It is, as Price said, a corrective. It seeks to dislodge rather than extend the conditions of a dominating stasis. Whenever it discerns a fixed composition, it knows that power is being exerted to pre- serve the organized pattern. Stasis is symptomatic of a situation in need of stimulation, or irritation. This opposition, however, does not attack its rival simply to replace its system for another. Rather the Picturesque insists on a continuous fluidity with irregularly spaced islands of control.

Lancelot Brown's successful landscape practice epitomized

system for Price and Knight. The similar gardens he produced in different parts of England clearly showed he was not a "judicious improver," one who knows when, and how, to deviate from any method, however generally good. The extent of Brown's effect elicited this lament from "a gentleman, whose taste and feeling, both for art and nature, rank as high as any man's: ...'This fellow crawls like a snail all over the grounds, and leaves his cursed slime behind him wherever he goes.'"

Even the language used to describe a Brownian landscape, both before construction to reassure the gentleman about to spend the money and after installation to give direction on how to see it, is "smooth, flowing and even-toned." The "proser" speaking these "common-place nothings" is the "very emblem of serpentine walks, belts and rivers, and all Mr. Brown's works." Of course the style of the true advocate of the Picturesque is quite the opposite. His speech is "full of unexpected turns,—of flashes of light: objects the most familiar, are placed by him in such singular, yet natural points of view,—he strikes out such unthought of agreements and con-trasts,—such combinations, so little obvious, yet never forced or affected, that the attention cannot flag." One eagerly listens for what is to come next instead of having one's soul tired out. It is not surprising that this description was ridiculed by those who saw in picturesque images nothing but capricious irritation.

Price and Knight, suspicious of system, cast a wary eye on each other, as well. When Knight describes Price's conception of beauty as a doctrine of innate ideas defining certain visible qualities as "beautiful," he discerns a "love of system." He accuses Burke of a similar attachment. Price turns around to see system in Knight's trains of association. Their shared wariness of any hint of the dreaded regularity of organization indicates how seriously they took the matter.

The adversaries, ostentation and vanity, produced a systemat-ic desire for obvious and recurrent display. Unmistakable regularity was the result of power sufficiently strong not to be missed, and not so limited as to exhaust itself in one or two manifestations. Land-owners, some of them recently installed in their estates, insisted that their country houses display the same regularity as the sacred architecture of the ancients, rather than the more adaptable examples of domestic buildings. "The system of regularity, of which the moderns have been so tenacious in the plans of their country houses, was taken from the sacred, and not from the domestic architecture of the ancients." Temples from Egypt, Greece, and Rome concentrated the desire for certainty and presented it in forms that aspired to the eternal. Domestic buildings of the ancients, by contrast, adjusted to the uses, the resources, and the inhabitants. System was the expression and the satisfaction of a desire for obvious control.

The question that finally must be answered by the Picturesque is what unsystematic connection can preserve liberty while avoiding both tyranny and license? The answer must be grounded on an important assumption about the relative scale of the composition. The duration of any plan of connection must either be short in relation to some conventional idea of a persisting totality, or of so long a duration as never to be completely grasped. For Knight, this is achieved "if the proprietor improve, not by a preconcerted plan, but by the more safe and certain method of gradual experiment." Such a way of making organizational choices emphasizes the pragmatic side of the Picturesque, which, in itself, is insufficient guide to the use of the power. In an effort to provide some kind of guide to what would otherwise become a totally unconnected sequence, Price suggests that Picturesque curves, "however they may approach regularity, never fall into [it]." Regular geometries are only to serve as asymptotes. Castiglione's admonition to the courtier-in-training that he learn to play the lute so as never to quite exhibit perfection would seem to be a similar practice. In all cases there is a gap between the composition and some obvious ideal of completion. The picturesque composition is positioned in relation to the ideal of compact, resistant identity even as it turns away from it.

This identity is formed by the plenitude that precedes the Picturesque.

How much interruption, or lack of completion, a clearly
shaped and carefully selected composition can support before it is
so compromised as to exhibit a totally mysterious chaos is the point
of balance that the Picturesque is eternally trying to locate.

True to its mediating origins, the Picturesque tries to avoid
two extremes of compositional regularity. On the one side is
smoothness. An excess of connection between the parts so blurs
their identity that only the whole is evident. At the other end is the
"want of connection—a passion for making everything distinct and
separate." The Picturesque occupies the position where one finds "a
pleasing and connected whole, though with detached parts." Power
and resources are not to be distributed in a picturesque composition
by savage variation and widely separated concentrations. When
differences are too great, connection must leap over the chasm. The
abrupt variation of picturesque aesthetics is not the gentle slope of
the Beautiful, nor is it the towering cliffs of the Sublime, but is more
like stair steps constructed to achieve elevation (or descent) by
incremental means. The parallels between these two opposing compositional categories and the political categories of tyranny and
license are never far from discussions of the Picturesque.

The balance between parts and whole is largely achieved by
means of "small connecting ties and bonds." If the parts of a composition are to retain their identities, then the connections with
other parts must be achieved by means of elements that function
specifically as linkages. However trifling these bonds may appear in
scenery, "they are those by which the more considerable objects in
all their different arrangements are combined, and on which their
balance, their contrast, and diversity, as well as union depends." In
the constant search for ways to make this point, Price reaches over
into the structure of language to say: "It would be hardly less absurd
to throw out all the connecting particles in language, as unworthy
of being mixed with the higher parts of speech. Our pages would

then be a good deal like our place, when all the conjunctions, prepositions, & c. were cleared away, and the nouns and verbs clumped by themselves."

The most often cited means to achieve the balance between the parts and the whole operates at the level of experience itself, and, it must be said, on an experience for the first time. As more than one commentator noticed, the novelty of a picturesque landscape works once, but not twice, or not in the same way. In so far as the landscape was a sequence of views, the composition did not work if one came in at the wrong end, for instance.

Curiosity, stimulated by partial concealments, keeps the extent and composition of the whole uncertain. Each successive part, therefore, has a distinct status because its place in a larger whole cannot be immediately grasped. Curiosity also serves to keep the experience in motion and stimulates the animation so beloved by the advocates of the Picturesque. It prevents the smoothness of familiarity from taking over. "Partial concealments are no less the sources of connection, than of variety, effect and intricacy."

Partial concealments, or absences, providing the "small connecting ties," is a striking notion. They keep the possiblity of a whole composition in mind as they propel the search for it, and at the same time they provide the distinctness of each successive part. Price refers these ties that are "reciprocally combined" to an example where the connection between water and land is so imperceptible "that in many places the eye cannot discover the perfect spot and time of their union; yet is no less delighted with that mystery."

"Connection is the very essence of the art of improvement." The emphasis on the relation between things, not the things themselves, determines whether the composition will operate more by linking parts into the whole or by making a distinction between parts. The sources for connection are found in the bonds between the parts in the compositions, in nature and in the workings of the mind, particularly as found in paintings. Finding the proper balance in a case-by-case activity is not easy, Price acknowledges. There is "no small difficulty in uniting breadth with detail." Breadth is the term borrowed from painting that describes the integrity of the whole composition. The steps that the composition takes to get from part to whole, or from " the inferior parts" to the principle, is through "their different gradation." This graded relationship insures variety as much as it contributes consequence or importance.

The composer creates the properly balanced composition by learning "to separate, to select and combine." This procedure, if not to say system, is unmistakably a human activity. Nature's elements are not simply imitated, but are rearranged according to combinations not necessarily found there. Separation suggests that an existing natural connection is not ratified or obeyed.

The new combination of nature's elements is exemplified by paintings which separate "what was most striking and well combined, from the less interesting and scattered objects of general scenery." The connections that may be diffused in "general scenery" are concentrated by "principles on which the effect of all visible objects must depend."

Writers on the Picturesque sought to illustrate compositions that did not suffer from the excess either of too much smooth unification or of too much scattered distinctness by looking to natural events as well as human creations. Greek temples are beautiful; they are systematically conceived and symmetrical. They become Picturesque when they are in ruins. Time is the "great author" of the changes that convert a beautiful object into a picturesque one. The Picturesque in this instance is once again dependent on the preexistence of a concentrated, obvious representation of control. The weather stains, partial incrustations and mosses interrupt the uniformity of surface and color by introducing roughness and variety of tint. The loosened stones tumble down and become mixed and overgrown with plants.

the presence of time in the environment suggests local control?

By admitting contrast and variety, the Gothic architects permitted more active trains of association. The resulting connections were fluid and variable. Greek architecture suffered from its obvious symmetry while Gothic architecture concealed its symmetry by the intricacy of its parts. Its composition did not obey any precise rules or restrictions. Its variety could be approached in different ways "since the acquisition of new ideas may at any time produce new associations, or change those previously existing." The nearly independent nature of the parts invites the close attention of immediate experience continuously reviewed and adjusted.

The more fashionable commentators, such as William Mason, took notice of the current delight in the Gothic as a way to describe how the picturesque composition could be formed. For him the Gothic harmony was the result of "disunited parts." "One majestic whole" was formed from small shapes "at once distinct and blended." The strong perception that takes a Gothic cathedral in at a glance can imagine that the harmony it finds there was produced in the same comprehensive act that discovered it. The problem for all the theorists of the Picturesque was to counterfeit the effects of time in an intentional compositional act. William Gilpin asked this very question: "whether it be possible for a single hand to build a picturesque village. Nothing contributes more to it than the various styles in building, which result from the different ideas of different people." The result is a particular kind of texture comprised of a sufficient number of singular identities distributed over a field. The connection between parts that seemed evident in the act of perception could be described in some way, but the means to achieve that result in a much more focused and compressed time frame of creation could not be satisfactorily described.

In discussing the architecture of Greek temples, Gothic abbeys and feudal castles, Price falls back on fairly classical ideals of adaption to "uses, circumstances, and situations," where the parts are "subservient to the purposes of the whole" and the ornaments are suited to the parts and to those making use of the building.

Should an English nobleman wish to make use of these precedents, "such changes and modifications should be admitted as may adapt to existing circumstances." If those modifications are made in the name of historical accuracy, the degree of exactitude becomes a measure of incongruity and the degree of deviation from fidelity a measure of responsiveness to principle, in a perfectly picturesque twist.

The looseness of picturesque compositions permitted a closer adjustment to functional requirements than the absolute control of a consistently applied system. Knight saw that when he noted how the Picturesque has the advantage of "being capable of receiving alterations and additions in almost any direction, without injury to its genuine and original character." A century and a half later in his talk to the Royal Insitute of British Architects on the connections between the Picturesque and Modernist Functionalism, Nikolaus Pevsner pointed out the same advantage. The familiar paradox—To be true is to deviate; to be exact is to be incongruous—arises immediately in any consideration of the Picturesque.

Picturesque correction of a systematically arranged composition could be effected through the application or, more aptly, toleration of pragmatic or functional considerations. A country house could escape an excess of smooth unification achieved by means of regular front and sides if the owner "were to insist upon having many of the windows turned towards those points where the objects were most happily arranged." The architect's response to such considerations would be to invent "a number of picturesque forms and combinations which otherwise might never have occurred to him; and would be obliged to do what so seldom has ever been done—to accommodate his building to the scenery, not to make that give way to his building."

We must remember that Price and Knight are clear that their application of picturesque principles is to be made in country houses, not city houses. "Architecture in towns may be said to be principle and independent." The presence of other human constructions in the city is not a context of difference, but of similarity. In the country, the setting, and therefore the issue of connection, is paramount. Compared to nature, architecture "is in some degree subordinate and dependent on the surrounding objects." The architect in the country is not just building with reference to other architecture past and present, but must work out the central issue of connection knowing that "each different situation requires a different disposition of the several parts." Thoughtful consideration of this extra responsibility will make it seem "as if some great artist had designed both the building and the landscape, they peculiarly suit and embellish each other."

[margin handwriting: seems like P. Theorists were headed toward Cezanne]

[margin handwriting: again, this is the issue of inherent structural logic of painting]

Nature provides examples of picturesque compositions as well. Taking the Picturesque as the expression of power underutilized, Price gives a wonderful example of how minimal intervention, or control exercised in a small, even inadvertent, way creates the proper pattern. "There is often a sort of spirit and animation in the manner in which old neglected pollards stretch out their immense limbs, . . . This careless method of cutting, just as the farmer happened to want a few stakes or poles, gives infinite variety to the general outline." The appearance of the trees was not the focus of the energy expended. Carelessness is not part of the intention of cutting the stakes. Calculation extended as far as cutting them, but not to the appearance of the tree after the cut, or the accumulation of a number of cuts. The spontaneity so beloved by the adherents of the Picturesque refers only to the subsequent visual effect of the pragmatic act of cutting. The mixture present in the situation is not only a visual one, but appears in the various intentions of farmer and observer. The one element in nature that seems to sum up picturesque composition is a tree, not bounded figures like human or animal bodies. A tree is "perhaps the only object where a grand whole, or at least what is most conspicuous in it, is chiefly composed of innumerable and distinct parts."

[margin handwriting: mixture in intentions]

The articulated visual field of a tree at one distance of viewing or a forest at another distance constitutes—along with waves, grass, clouds, and herds of animals, all parts of a landscape scene—a surface whose system of development is not immediately discernible. The Picturesque is trying to describe a way to produce such aesthetic objects. The desire to create them may arise from some very primordial urge to connect with an original chaos or from a very sophisticated interpretation and representation of that imagined beginning. To use another example from Japan, the monk's robe of poverty that is thought to have been worn by Shotoku Taishi, the prince who is considered the founder of Buddhism in Japan in the sixth century A.D., is an amazing composition (although one is reluctant even to use the word except to describe its physical act of making) of irregular patches of silk overlapped in layers of soft, naturally dyed colors of chestnut brown, ocher, and dulled forest green. This kind of robe, called "distant mountains," has fragments worn away to reveal in part the layers underneath like mist thinning to reveal ranges of receding peaks. As an example of picturesque composition, one could hardly ask for more: the minute parallel lines of stitches that tie the floating scraps into a rationalized whole, the avoidance of the orthogonal regularity of warp or weft when cutting the fragments and the transformation of silk into rags to be worn by a member of the royal court who, according to the Buddha's list of sources for the fabric, could very well have donated the cloth which now reappears on his back as a symbol of poverty.

With painting as a major focus of the way to make picturesque compositions, the effects of light during the day and in various seasons provide instructive examples. Winter light, because it is predominantly horizontal, even at mid-day, produces lights and shadows that "finely illuminate the parts," while providing fullness and connection. The autumn sun, because it follows a low course above the horizon compared with the higher summer sun, which is a "vague and general glare of light without shadow," also produces lights and shadows that resemble late afternoon and evening during a much larger portion of the day. Price does not cite the symmetrical height of the sun after dawn, or in spring, almost as if he knew that the Picturesque comes after fullness, not before.

Colors as well can contribute to the picturesque version of "wholeness," and of course they are autumnal hues, used with such effect by the Venetian school, "particularly that of Giorgione and Titian, which has been the great object of imitation." Venice, itself, although it is not singled out for any extended discussion, is a rich fabric of mixture as the careful aristocratic traders mixed new construction with old in their palace/storehouses merged by the flickering waters of the Grand Canal.

If a compositional mode is "promiscuous" enough, it is difficult to say when it is operating and when it is not. Its limits or boundaries are difficult to ascertain and "it is on the shape, and disposition of its boundaries, that the picturesque, must, in great measure, depend." Lacking a core or center because it is about relationships on its edges, the Picturesque seems to cast itself adrift by avoiding questions of origin.

The dominant mode of improvement, against which the Picturesque set its metaphors of mixture and abrupt variation, can be comprehended as a whole immediately. "If you traverse it in every direction, little new can occur." While in a picturesque composition, "every step changes the whole of the composition." Lacking a stable center that one can occupy with assurance, the Picturesque requires continuous movement.

Progression becomes a sine qua non for creating a picturesque composition. The most rational way to imitate the happy effects of "the *progressive* state of nature which we *now* observe, is to observe the manner in which she progressively creates them, and instead of prescribing to her a set form, from which she must not presume to vary, we ought so to prepare everything that her efforts may point out, what, without such indications, we never can suggest to ourselves." To propose that we include the operation of natural forces into our compositions because their progression cannot be calculated abdicates the total control that other compositions require.

A good bit of the controversy surrounding the Picturesque at the turn of the nineteenth century was directed at its definition, its boundaries. William Gilpin embodied the simplest notion in his pencil sketches and the observations he made while drawing. Price and Knight argued with each other and with Humphrey Repton over the definition of the term. Differences turned on niceties of philosophical argument as well as on what each individual's taste was willing to include in the category as he understood it. As a middle term between Burke's Beautiful and Sublime, the Picturesque shifted uneasily between two powerful poles.

The possibility of making some rules to describe the Beautiful and the Sublime seemed within the reach of many commentators on aesthetic matters. As limiting conditions, there seemed some point to defining the absolute characteristics of the two aesthetic categories at the extreme edge. Standing in between these poles, looking at the aesthetic material closer at hand, the definition of an aesthetic category such as the Picturesque becomes more difficult. At the immediate distance of individual perception distinctions became critical and what lay in the perceiving mind more important. At this scale, it seemed as though discrimination became an individual matter.

The problem for a compositional mode that emphasizes small-scale elements is found in the question, What organizes them in a whole? For example, George Mason recommended variety between groups of trees, but not within a group. For him, then, the "group" of trees was an irreducible whole when seen as part of a broad landscape composition. The distance from which any composition is viewed determines what is a part and what is a whole. The landscape paintings usually referred to as models for landscape gardening were taken from a certain viewpoint. At that aesthetic distance, a "group" of trees was a discernible unit in the picture frame.

Mason insisted on the distinction between contrast and incongruity as did Jacques de Lille, who observed that "contrast and

contradiction differ far." Contrast was the central organizing principle of the Picturesque. Contrast was achieved by incorporating
roughness, irregularity, and abrupt variation in a situation that
lacked them. What saved it from simply being an assemblage of
contradictory parts was a connection that the Picturesque both
suspected and required.

Novelty and "abrupt variation" are the primary parts of the
Picturesque argument undermining the connection that makes any
obvious composition. Novelty is the impact on the observer's mind
of a stimulus that departs from what is expected. But what is novel
to one may not be unexpected to another. And, more significantly,
what is novel once may be expected the second time. The spectator's state of mind, whose importance eighteenth-century "psychological philosophy" such as Stewart and Alison pursued, became the
isolated location of sensibility.

The path along existing natural features in a picturesque garden often provided connection without the designer having to
supply it. This was the case in Shenstone's Leasowes and Morris's
Persfield among others. Even if the natural features were "modestly
ministered" to by design, the linkage, the compositional connection
between the parts was made by the path, the abstract line of
connection followed by the mobile perception. Abrupt variation
also breaks the continuity of any systematic composition. No sooner does a pattern get started, than the Picturesque breaks into its
predictability with other stimuli that may obey a different pattern
or may simply be unique, unattached events. Knight included in his
Progress of a Civil Society the observation that "A partial discord lends
its aid to tie / The complex knots of general harmony."

The most obvious connection between parts of a composition
is provided by possessing them. Owning a landscape or a building
made its parts equally related to whoever possessed them. In fact,
this rather gross connection may be a substitute for many other,
internal patterns. Polite imagination relates any prospect to itself
by making it "a kind of property." Satisfaction is gained by possess-

ing a scene without requiring ownership in fact. Being satisfied by virtual possession comes more easily to one whose plate is already full. Only if the "taint" of desire is absent is the trick of aesthetic contemplation completely successful. The ability to imagine a relationship to a landscape without taking possession of it is not given to the "generality of Mankind." When one who exercises polite imagination is able to make "the most rude uncultivated Parts of Nature administer to his Pleasures," he is discovering a "Multitude of Charms" that are concealed from ordinary people.

As Knight's lines above indicated, connection made between parts without the use of system also applied to political compositions. Knight wrote on Fox's death in 1806 that his singular contribution was working for the "general cause," especially by being vigilant of ambition and corruption. The general cause is served by mitigating the extremes either of weakness or rashness. Knight saw Fox working to "connect the parts, and animate the whole." For him, Fox recognized that "one Almighty universal soul / Lives in each part and regulates the whole." The attention paid to the matter of connection kept the political situation from breaking up. The general cause needed establishment, while at the same time the parts that contributed to it needed the freedom to act.

The risks that Fox and others ran who acted according to principles of mixture and not pressing an advantage was the absence of a clear tradition of composition compounded over time. Horace Walpole's estimation of Fox pointed to this very problem. "Nature had given him genius and to her he left it to furnish him with occasions of displaying it. . . . He acted as the moment impelled him . . . yet might have advantaged himself and his country more, had he acted with any foresight or any plan."

The lineaments that run through a complex picturesque mixture produce a union that must remain somewhat undefined. The classical ideal of balance that still operates in the Picturesque locates it as a hinge between the enlightenment and the romanticism of the nineteenth century. "Balanced interests" is one way that

Knight tried to characterize the connection between the parts of a republic. In such an entity "self-balanced rights" linked part to part. The poise of these "self-constituted" parts was superior to the condition "when, with rule and line, / Vain prescience passion's limits would define." Knight is struggling to find a way to suggest that the relationships between the parts in a political composition are self-determined and yet not at war with each other. The terms of the peace are powerful, yet anything but obvious. What he is sure will not work is to define the terms of the connection between the political parts in a systematic or regular way. Just as in recommendations for aesthetic compositions, "rule and line" are the specific tyrannies that must be avoided. In a metaphor that recalls Isaac Newton, Knight uses a mechanical image to characterize the connection between parts of the society: "The separate classes act as springs and weights."

Knight's *Progress of a Civil Society* continues the argument first proposed in his poem *The Landscape* that there was a connection between the structure of landscape design and the structure of society. In Book IV these lines reinforce the similarities he perceived:

> As when in formal lines, exact and true,
> The pruner's scissors shear the ductile yew,
> Amused, its shape and symmetry we see,
> But seek in vain the likeness of a tree;
> And while the artist's pleasing skill we trace,
> Lament the loss of every native grace:
> So when too strictly social habits bind,
> The native vigour of the roving mind,
> Pleased, the well-ordered system we behold,
> Its justly regulated parts unfold,
> But search in vain its complicated plan,
> To find the native semblance of a man;
> And, 'midst the charms of equal rule, deplore
> The loss of graces art can ne'er restore.

This passage contains one of the uncertainties of Knight's argument. The opposition between "equal rule" and "native grace" is clear. "Grace" is the visual evidence that nature enjoys mixture. Departures from the formal line that man's art uses to understand or rectify nature is no longer a defect, but the sign of the critical difference between the two methods of composition. "True wisdom" is shown "by modest doubt." The presence of doubt in a *Protestant position* compositional scheme presents a problem that we have encountered before. Its existence in the composition raises the question of what it is we are looking at. The composition's status is not completely asserted by its presence. The doubt reaches out of the composition to the person attending to it and initiates a questioning that is at the heart of the Picturesque. Clearly the composer could tidy up the composition, but he chooses not to.

In this passage Knight is also working on two levels when he refers to the "complicated plan" that the artist has presented. Complexity would seem to be characteristic of a composition that included mixture and doubt. Yet complication is apparently evidence of the "formal lines," "exact and true" of a "well-ordered system." The way nature composes is more direct, therefore simpler, than the tyrannical artist whose imposition of equal rule is possible only by intricate interventions that confine the graces of nature. The connection that regulates civil societies is also "strong though concealed." Growths, irregularities, and doubt give political regulation its resilience. Whether one reads concealment as one more instance of behind-the-scenes manipulation by an "unseen hand" or as the unrationalized growth resulting from inescapably human contradictions is one way to decide whether the Picturesque is threatening or benign.

When Price suggests that there is a place in picturesque landscape design for the use of obviously constructed elements like stone paths bounded by walls, he is not reversing the progress away from the formal hegemony of an earlier era, but is demonstrating that the Picturesque is about connections between things, in this case the loose variety of nature and the rule of human structure, rather than the things themselves. In his description of a walk by the house, a crucial linkage between man and nature, he starts with the reasonable requirement that the walk be "broad and dry." Although there has been a change from stone to gravel in current practice, that is not the point. What is important is "their immediate boundaries." The line of the modern gravel walk's edge of mown grass is "meagre, formal and insipid," even if it is obscured by the spread of low shrubs or grass. The connection between the house and the lawn is made flat and unvaried by the absence of a firmly formed transition. The result is not rich or picturesque, but slovenly. The older style of paved terrace when bounded by a simple parapet wall of cut stone "has a finished and determined form, together with a certain massiveness which is wanting to the other." The contrast of its color with that of the vegetation provides the linking distinctness that painters always include.

Principles of connection that are clearly understood and employed by artist or politician have a reassuring certainty. They can be understood and taught. Picturesque connection is unsteady and may be unreliable. When William Mason quotes William Temple in a note in Book I of his poem *The English Garden*, he points out the risk taken by compositions similar to the Picturesque. It is "a too hardy achievement for common hands; and tho' there may be more honour if they succeed well, yet there is more dishonour if they fail, and it is twenty to one they will, whereas in regular figures it is hard to make any great and remarkable faults." The question of making a mistake composing according to picturesque principles presupposes there is a way of making such a distinction. To render that judgment there must be a determinable boundary which contains the composition, a point at which one includes the phenomena organized according to a compositional rule and a point beyond it which does not. Getting it right within that boundary means achieving some pattern that distinguishes itself from the surroundings.

When, and at what scale, the compositional test is applied distinguishes picturesque compositions from more formal examples. Because the Picturesque is a continuously adjusting arrangement, its "success" must be closer to a statistical average than an absolute judgment.

The contribution that mental processes make to connection was also part of the theory of the Picturesque. Trying to incorporate the new psychological ideas into traditional notions of beauty led some commentators to seek a balance between them. William Mason could say that "Grace is caught by strong perception, not from rules" and a few lines later recommend that trees be trimmed twice a year "when ever some random branch has strayed / Beyond the bounds of beauty." Rule clearly is something imposed on individual citizens and individual natural objects. A strong perception is a kind of rule unto itself that can, from its own repertoire of experiences, make a structure of associations that organize its own aesthetic moments. Only when the rule that regulates the aggregate is "chaste" can benevolence displace tyranny. Payne Knight advanced the associationist model to explain how the Picturesque worked as a collection of stimuli operating on a collection of previous experiences. When his *Inquiry* was reviewed in the first decade of the nineteenth century, this perceptual aspect of his argument seemed particularly important. The *British Critic* noted in January and February 1807 that it was "good to analyse what belongs to the eye and what to some other sense or faculty" in what was "commonly called 'the association of ideas.'" And *The Critical Review* summarized Knight's argument: "to show how far the pleasures of mere organic sensation extend, and to separate these pleasures from such as are derived from the operation of the mind."

In his chapter on uniformity and variety composed in 1753, Lord Kames considered the rate of perceptual stimulation. He quotes John Locke when observing that connection is perceived when the succession of apprehension is fast while disconnection is preceived when it is slow. Slow trains emphasize variety, fast ones reveal an overall pattern. Based on the rapidity with which the apprehension of the object can be made, a natural scene, then, has greater variety than a painting which, in turn, has more than a verbal description. In Joseph Craddock's novel *Village Memoires* (1775) the pace of perceptions is clearly one way to distinguish good gardens from bad. In the view of the conservative village clergyman writing to his son, gardens must exhibit a great and singular plan to a rapid, overall view that can only be slowed down by "foreign conceits," which mislead the observer "into another sort of pleasure opposite to that which is designed in the general plan." The momentum of perception that brings the plan to completion, which is the designer's aim, is slackened by diversions. The viewer so misled is locked up "like a knight-errant in an enchanted castle, when he should be pursuing his main adventure." Jacques de Lille also urged the gardener to let "motion be first your care" and immediately links this perceptual motion to political ideals: "If life and motion thus delight the eye, / It loves no less an air of liberty."

When the plenitude of motion becomes a criterion for the picturesque compositional ideal, the extreme case of congestion appears. Separating mixture from congestion is one of the functions of connection in picturesque compositions. Both mere mixture and underutilization of resources can produce the confusion avoided by the Picturesque and abhorred as the inevitable end of such promiscuousness by its enemies.

The connection of parts that have been liberated remained an elusive goal for the Picturesque; elusive if one requires a simple, persisting description of how parts are arranged into a composition. It may be that stating the problem of connection, not its resolution, was the important point to be made by the Picturesque. If nothing else, the Picturesque preferred continuous adjustment, review, re-definition over any illusion of certainty. The adjustments apparently settle into a compensating binary oscillation as liberty seeks to correct the polar extremes of license and tyranny. If so, then a system seems to emerge.

A natural system of compensation as energy flows continuously in search of an entropic conclusion may, at last, underlie the
open-ended artifice of the Picturesque. Such an appeal to nature is
an easy one to make, as we have seen from the comments from the
eighteenth century. But the recombination of elements given by
nature, that is, human artifice, is a way out of such a mechanical
pendulum swing even with the suspicion that a continuous reframing of the pattern at successively larger or smaller scales will simply
uncover a cosmic pattern of repetition.

The conclusion may be closer to dear William Shenstone's
speculation that these compositional difficulties appear simply because we eternally live on a margin where incomplete patterns are
all we have as the background for our diminutive efforts at com-
pleteness. The provisional character of picturesque composition
sets up a vulnerable situation. By cultivating uncertainty, the Picturesque is open to conquest by those who rush to assume a completion to our marginal location in the cosmos. Such a proposition
forgets, however, that the Picturesque is not an answer, it is a way
of calling to task any assertion that enforces its effect by means of
a self-perpetuating system.

key element - such
systems limit diversity
in politics -

PROSPECT

After all, this patchwork of the Picturesque leaves us wondering how something so vexing, so elusive can have become so thin and dismissible. To call something Picturesque these days is generally to render it weak and superficial. The complexity demonstrated above has been reduced to some very simple patterns of visual stimuli replicated over and over in our world of instantaneous representation. Maybe the Picturesque is the natural way of seeing in a time when technology produces increasingly sophisticated pictures that approximate the depth of reality. Holograms and computer imaging may be the ultimate proof of insights two hundred years old.

The Picturesque tried to figure out a way to arrange the parts of a composition, not by tyrannical imposition and not by giving up hope of making any kind of stable composition at all. It was a stage in Donald Lowe's *History of Bourgeois Perception*. The Picturesque stands at the hinge between "estate culture" and "bourgeois culture." It tried to reconcile, at least momentarily, a passing world based on nontemporal, static classification with an emerging one that emphasized transformation and focused on structure rather than taxonomy. The increasing mobility of ideas, people, and resources required a level of abstraction and placelessness that the specifics of the land could no longer support. A generalized system of laws necessarily suppressed the unique aspects of any case in favor of a universalizing sense of justice. The Picturesque tried to mediate between both cultures by having the estate tell us about mobility.

The Picturesque's distaste for leveling and its desire to preserve distinctness asserted the localized wisdom of the estate to thwart universalizing abstraction. But the emphasis on relationship, on edges and boundaries between categories, aligned the Picturesque with the forces leading to a bourgeois culture. Gardens that once served as the transition from an economy of wood and water to one of iron and coal, from estate culture to bourgeois culture may yet show how to make the transition from bourgeois culture to electronic culture.

Through their dependency on a surplus of wealth, education, or spiritual commitment, the Picturesque and the pastoral can assume a posture of relaxed underutilization of power. Just as the pastoral was a carefree interlude away from the closely defined propriety at court, the Picturesque can be seen, in Lowe's terms, as a "perceptual field centered in towns and radiated outward." It depends on the concentrated accumulation of convention as its object. The pastoral cannot exist without the metropolis, neither can the Picturesque exist without the apparently inevitable tendency of power to centralize. Whether the city can exist without the Picturesque is a question some would have no trouble answering in the affirmative, but such a city would fall victim to an illusion of stability that the Picturesque is specifically designed to question.

As Italo Calvino muses through his character Mr. Palomar at the Ryoanji garden near Kyoto: "Must the conclusion be that the Zen mental techniques for achieving extreme humility, detachment from all possessiveness and pride, require as their necessary background aristocratic privilege, and assume an individualism with so much space and so much time around it, the horizon of a solitude free of anguish."

The Picturesque takes place in an interval of subsidence. It is located in the gap between full utilization of all resources and an apparently rustic poverty. When a complete composition is within reach because the means to reach it are not in doubt and do not need to be tested, in other words, when completion is not at risk, the Picturesque can hold back. The resulting space has a very special quality, like Tityrus's protected farm in Virgil's First Eclogue.

It is a relaxed art that looks askance at any obsessive acquisitiveness. Its risk is not the result of capitalist speculation, but of being misrepresented. By challenging the drive for completion as a vain protection against uncertainty, the Picuresque eases off control in the interest of alternative readings.

The gap of subsidence produces the plenitude required by the Picturesque. Plenitude can be spiritual and intellectual as well as material, as has been noted before. This suggests that it is not an absolute condition, but a relative one. Any subsidence can produce a kind of plenitude. Tityrus's composure, in Virgil's First Eclogue, is not opulent. He did not go to Rome to be made a prince; he sits piping much as he did as a shepherd. Whether he employs his ease to engage in indulgent self-satisfaction, in critical reflection, or in an irritating mix of the two, determines the fruitfulness of the plenty. The challenge of detecting the subsidence in such a scene makes the Picturesque anything but obvious to an observer.

The plenitude of subsidence can be chosen, but it can also be suffered. The resources necessary for completing a composition can be consciously withheld; they are available to be taken up but are artfully laid aside. Someone without the option of taking up those resources can still produce a picturesque composition by cultivating the gap they can no longer close. That is the condition of ruins or of lives deprived of those resources. Aristocratic seediness or noble poverty are unmistakably Picturesque. The Picturesque can also be induced, so to speak, by asserting that a point of completion and control is available, when, in fact, it cannot be reached. The interval between the assertion and the actual control of resources becomes virtual plenitude.

Subsidence is open to the charge of complacency. Not to use all one's resources seems an unproductive posture, almost accepting inevitable decline, like living off the legacy of a rougher, earlier time, a position not very different from the gentlemen commentators on the Picturesque of the eighteenth century. The plenitude enjoyed by Price and Knight was not of long standing, two generations at most, but it was long enough to pass beyond the comfort of possession to entertain an artful subsidence from it. The direct exercise of entreprenurial risk is one way to produce new plenitude; tolerating a vagrant drift in a picturesque interval of subsidence is another. The Picturesque recognizes these alternatives through the intermittency that saves it from any claims of totality, or of self-sufficiency. Like the contrasts of sensory stimuli, the Picturesque is only for a while, depending on the circumstances. It moves; it is suspense, novelty, and pursuit.

The Picturesque is virtually invisible to those who believe concentrations of power are eternal. When they come upon picturesque subsidence, they can only "take it straight." The doubt, the irritating uncertainty of the Picturesque completely escapes committed despots. One of the most striking proofs of this fact is the action that the Nazis took when they came upon a bridge in a palace garden outside Berlin. This bridge, built by an apprentice of Karl Friedrich Schinkel, crossed over an artificial waterway fed by a pump-driven waterfall. Its three and a half stone arches spanned only part way over the stream. The remaining gap was spanned by wooden planks. In the 1930s the Nazis repaired the "damage" by "completing" the masonry structure. Despotism cannot take any risks; any system working at full bore has no unused plenitude with which to amuse itself or entertain irony.

Concern about one's status, worry over risks to one's identity ultimately find their way into discussions about composition: aesthetic, political, whatever. Picturesque subsidence is not an ultimate, metabolic risk; it operates in terms of how we represent ourselves to ourselves and to each other. Engaging in picturesque compositions makes definition of the subject difficult. Working through that difficulty can be risked only if one does not feel so vulnerable as to lose one's self in the process. The achievement of a self that does not aim at a final state is the precondition of letting loose. Looseness, or promiscuity, is the pejorative aspect of being able to engage in critical reflection, especially of recently acquired resources. The critique of reading, its control and limitation, its separation from "direct experience," is useful to one who reads, but it is absolutely destructive to one who does not. Picturesque rough-ness comes after smoothness, not before.

it's not developmental

The gap between the task or composition at hand and the excess of resources available is the direct antithesis of a pragmatic or functionalist approach to composition. The tight congruence of task and resources is effective only in a situation of general consensus of what is to be done. The plentitude required by the Picturesque is a recognition of the fact that the operation of power always means conflict. The freedom to explore alternatives, to adjust frames of reference, to engage in rhetoric in the interest of composing conflict is produced by this gap between the power available and the size of the compositional task at hand.

As long as the pastoral and the Picturesque engage in skirmishes around the edges of the citadel, as long as they do not presume to mount a frontal assault in order to replace its concentrated identity by fragmenting questions, they will be potent forces. Who makes the challenge is important. Picturesque irritation is not usually made by those who are totally marginal. An attack by those who have never known life in the citadel is not carried out as skirmishes, but as furious destruction. The picturesque and pastoral challenge is made by residents on vacation from the center who engage in a kind of shadow-boxing. As weekend vagabonds, or as gypsies in the last stages of cultural history outlined by the Renaissance architect and theoretician Alberti, the advocates of the Picturesque enrich a dominant tradition, mix it with doubt, but do not undermine it totally. It also enlists supporters from outside the walls whose taste for the Picturesque can be stimulated by visits or tours of the citadel.

When the Picturesque and the pastoral are used as escapes from the responsibilities of the city, they become perverse and sinister. One goes to the Picturesque as one goes on a picnic, heading away from the city on the way to a distant hillside. Upon arrival, the eyes are turned back on the city in a questioning glance. Should the gaze, in the mistaken form of a quest, be directed away from the city, the tension, doubt, and uncertainty will be lost. What may then appear as a peaceful garden is an illusion of exclusiveness that will eventually converge with its opposite locked up in the citadel.

The decline in the intellectual energy of the Picturesque since the eighteenth century is the story of a futile quest. Suburbia is its fleeting location where exclusion can be maintained only momentarily. The bourgeois appropriated the Picturesque by concentrating on its surfaces, by taking it "straight." The Picturesque is easy to misread, especially by those who aspire to control by manipulating appearances.

The problem of how to regulate a composition based on picturesque principles faced several generations of designers. Archaeological eclecticism was one mode used to control such a wayward attitude, as Colin Rowe has pointed out. But the Picturesque itself followed a different course. In part because they did not require consciousness of all the compensations and adjustments, the retinal stimulus patterns inevitably became dominant. Uvedale Price vainly fought that abbreviation. Composing according to its simplified rules of contrast, irregularity, and roughness made the Picturesque the victim of its own misunderstanding. By becoming a style that could be appropriated for social enjoyment, it quickly left behind its more demanding aspects.

The early stages of this devolution are evident in the 1804 collection entitled: "Views of Noblemen and Gentlemen's Seats, Antiquities, and Remarkable Buildings in the Counties Adjoining London." These descriptions, sounding for all the world like current Sunday real estate advertisements, are largely of places bought or improved by "merchants of respectability." One place began as a peasant's dwelling, was "purchased on speculation by an ingenious mechanic" from London who during the fifteen years of his ownership "employed his leisure hours" to exercise his "fancy in improvements." He presumably got a good price from Charles Walcot, Esq., who made it his family residence.

The description of Woodland Cottage, Clapham, Surrey, the seat of William Lynn, Esq., leads immediately into the common misunderstandings that the Picturesque suffered so easily.

"Retirement engages the affections of men, whenever it holds up a picture of tranquility to their view. 'The mind never feels with more energy and satisfaction that it lives, that it is rational, great, active, free, and immortal, than during those moments in which it excludes idle and impertinent intruders.' For this purpose, and to relax from the fatigues of professional employment, the proprietor erected this homely, yet elegant little cottage: a humble thatch covers its roof and a plain, unostentatious, but convenient fitting up, are its internal advantages... In the dining parlour, the modern Gothic is pursued; the table, chairs, wainscoting, and sideboard, resemble, in miniature, the ancient appearance of the hall of an old castle, to which the stained glass windows give a sombre finish." This summarizes the total rejection of the public realm. The view from this humble cottage is firmly fixed away from London. Its exclusiveness not only undermines itself, it puts the city in jeopardy as well.

The temptation to take it at its word, like reading Virgil unreflectively, set the Picturesque on a course of self-destruction almost immediately. Weekend visitors to a neighboring hamlet would take in the views while rummaging in their picnic baskets. Painting fences "sober olive green" may be taken as a way to disguise boundaries and limits, but it serves to conceal more troubling questions about artifice and nature in the interest of apparent freedom. After all is it not about ease and enjoyment?

A pattern of composition that requires continuous enactment and review, a category in the middle that redefines itself as time passes, as situations change, as contexts alter, is not comforting, but irritating. One of the ways to short-circuit its inherently challenging nature is to reduce its impact to the retina. The Picturesque is easily appropriated to make it consumable. To take it straight, to use its surface of simplicity and its appeals to nature's irreducibility so as to smooth out the perception of the layers that lie beneath, is the quickest way to make it a commodity. Once pictures are taken straight, are taken as blunt sensory instruments creating an impact that cannot be argued or subjected to skeptical review, then the deep questions to which the Picturesque mutely points are lost.

The marginalization of the Picturesque from both sides—the forces that build and preserve identities as well as the forces that break down all compositions into the smallest common denominator—puts it into an almost untenable position. It must fight to keep from disappearing as well as from prevailing. By reframing the composition, by making the former whole into a part, the Picturesque scans the whole range of possible compositions. It fitfully composes and re-composes, never settling on one boundary rather than another. Walt Whitman's most picturesquely composed poem "Song of Myself," trails off with the invitation: "Missing me one place, search another / I stop somewhere, waiting for you." The Picturesque is similarly elusive as a compositional achievement. Inquiring whether one is in its presence or not continuously re-enacts it.

The Picturesque tries to find a way to incorporate doubt into compositional activity. Its motley appearance is the result of questioning interruptions that serve as incremental self-corrections. As a corrective it concentrates on moments between vigorous acquisition and fertile dissolution.

Notes

PROLOGUE

PAGE xii   ". . .is the sign of real wealth": Italo Calvino, *If on a winter's night a traveler*, trans. William Weaver, 1981, p. 109.

MIXTURE

PAGE 1   ". . . mixed with the modern style": Uvedale Price, *On the Picturesque*, 1794, p. 305.
On Powis Castle, Price, 1842, p. 436.
". . . all is mixed and blended together": Price, 1796, p. 29.

PAGE 2   ". . . are perpetually mixed together": Price, 1796, p. 106.
". . . but admits of all promiscuously": Richard Payne Knight, *An Analytical Inquiry into the Principles of Taste*, 1805, p. 225.
On "old" gardens, Price, 1842, p. 300.

PAGE 3   ". . . airs of ease and playfulness": Price, 1842, p. 309.

PAGE 4   ". . . the Effect of Design": Joseph Addison, *Spectator*, essay 414.
". . . bearing their natural forms": Robert Castell, *Villas of the Ancients*, 1728.

PAGE 5   On the three qualities, Price, 1796, p. 61.

PAGE 6   ". . . lands between two cart-ruts": Price, 1842, p. 464.
On "opposite qualities": Price, 1796, p. 61.
"cut down ancient Vistas": William Mason, *The English Garden*, 1783, Book 1, line 333.

PAGE 7   ". . . an air of solitude," ". . . regularity and art," ". . . fine effect": Lord Kames, *Elements of Criticism*, 1762, pp. 301–3.
". . . pleasure which we originally felt": Knight, p. 22.

PAGE 8   ". . . hurrying, impetuous": Price, 1796, p. 146.
". . . the grace of novelty": William Shenstone, "Unconnected

Thoughts on Gardening," *The Works in Verse and Prose of William Shenstone, Esq.*, 1768, vol. 2, p. 95.

PAGE 9 ". . . decorations to advantage": Shenstone, p. 95.
". . . our fancy to the contrary": Shenstone, p. 98.
". . . Lustre through a whole sentence": Addison, *Spectator*, essay 421.
Longinus's sublime "flashing forth a thunderbolt": Peter de Bolla, *Discourse of the Sublime*, p. 37.

PAGE 10 ". . . a Picture of the greatest Variety": Addison, *Spectator*, essay 477.
"universal source of pleasure": Price, 1796, p. 25.

PAGE 11 ". . . mason-work as any in the country": Price, 1796, p. 213.
". . . ils font face partout": Price, 1796, p. 269.

PAGE 12 ". . . 'Clump your javelin men'": Price, 1796, p. 269, note.
"mechanical common-place operation." Price, 1796, p. 40.
"perpetual change without variety": Price, 1796, p. 270.
On the gardens of Wise and Le Nôtre, Addison, *Spectator*, essay 477.

PAGE 13 ". . . sinks into distaste and weariness": Price, 1796, p. 167.
". . . more wild and irregular": Price, 1842, p. 321, notes.
". . . melodies of a composer": Price, 1842, p. 204.
". . . metaphysical extravagancy": George Mason, *Essay on Design in Modern Gardening*, 1768, p. 155.
". . . a liberal understanding," ". . . some correspondent part of the other": George Mason, 1768, p. 155.

PAGE 14 ". . . chiefly taken from it": Price, 1796, p. 295 note.

PAGE 15 On the failed attempt at imitating Gothic, *Gentlemens Magazine* 67 (June 1797): 473–74.
". . . columns and entablatures within," ". . . and convenient dwelling": Knight, p. 223.
". . . Improvements every morning": Knight to Aberdeen, September 3, 1810, in *Arrogant Connoisseur*, ed. Michael Clark and Nicholas Penn, 1982.
"suit and embellish each other": Price, 1842, p. 328.

PAGE 16 ". . . radicalism with conservatism": A. S. Turberville, *A History of Welbeck Abbey and Its Owners*, 1939, p. 211.

". . . only to a mixed government": Charles James Fox, *A Set of Slips*, column 13, vol. iv, p. 52.

PAGE 17 "between beauty and sublimity": Price, 1842, pp. 90, 110, 510.

"blended, but perfectly distinct": Price, 1796, p. 82.

". . . horror of sublimity": Price, 1796, p. 105.

". . . to feel, to enjoy," ". . . the beautiful and the picturesque": Price, 1796, p. 104 note.

On an admixture, a corrective, Price, 1796, p. 105.

PAGE 18 ". . . flowing lines and colors," ". . . intellectual qualities of things": Knight, p. 75.

". . . his definition of Beauty": Dugald Stewart, *Philosophical Essays*, 1810, p. 74.

PAGE 19 When Price addressed the matter, Price, 1842, p. 360.

"doctrine and system": Price, 1842, p. 98.

PAGE 22 "supernatural sublimity," ". . . colloquial vulgarity": Knight, *The Progress of a Civil Society*, Preface.

". . . all my neighbors": Robert Potter, *Observations of the Poor Laws*, 1775, pp. 64–65 notes.

PAGE 23 ". . . cools fervor," ". . . and Fiction": Knight, *Progress*, l. 134.

". . . planned by prospective wisdom": Knight, *Progress*, l. 186.

". . .styles of improvement": Price, 1842, p. 375.

PAGE 25 ". . . neatness and convenience": Price, 1842, p. 455.

". . . equality is deformity": John Thomas Smith, "Remarks on Rural scenery with twenty etchings of cottages from Nature and some observations and precepts relative to the picturesque," 1797, p. 13.

PAGE 26 ". . . the eye and the mind": Price, 1842, p. 300.

". . . but excluded all others": Price, 1842, p. ix.

". . . a totally opposite nature," ". . . a highly cultivated mind": Price, 1842, p. 251.

PAGE 27 ". . . as in all other objects": Price, 1842, p. 338.

PASTORAL

PAGE 31 ". . . below their intellecual means": Bruno Snell, *The Discovery of the Mind*, trans. T. G. Rosenmeyer, 1953, p. 36.

PAGE 34 ". . . incompetence or deliberate artifice": W. V. Clausen, *Age of Augustus*, 1982, p. 12.

PAGE 36 ". . . in the heart of towns": Sannazaro, *Arcadia*, preface.
". . . imitates her imitator": Tasso, *Jerusalem Delivered*, canto 16, stanza 10.

PAGE 41 ". . . glance at larger matters": George Puttenham, *Art of English Poesie*, p. 29.

COMPOSITIONS OF POLITICS AND MONEY

PAGE 57 ". . . to a coal-and-iron basis": Phyllis Deane, *The First Industrial Revolution*, 1965, p. 129.

PAGE 59 ". . . to endanger the other two": A. S. Turberville, p. 47.

PAGE 61 ". . . a torrent of ideas," ". . . the sculptor's art": *Morning Post*, September 14, 1806, pp. 12–13.
". . . to all Mankind," ". . . Rights of the People": "The Speech of the R.H. Charles James Fox Declaring His Principles Respecting the Present Crisis of Public Affairs and a Reform in the Representation of the People."

PAGE 62 ". . . the Crown party here": Leslie George Mitchell, *Charles James Fox and the Disintegration of the Whig Party, 1782–94*, 1971, p. 236.
". . . fewer individual opinions": Fox, A Set of Slips, column 19, vol. v, p. 108.

PAGE 64 ". . . priviledges of the Commons": Mitchell, p. 229.
". . . argument to argument," ". . . strong hand of power": *Correspondence of Charles James Fox*, p. 34.
". . . more durable and firm," ". . . charity for those of others": *Correspondence of Charles James Fox*, p. 207.

PAGE 65 ". . . not by their thoughts": "Speech on the Repeal of the Test Laws," p. 29.

". . . open and liberal discussion": "Speech on the Repeal of the Test Laws," p. 34.

PAGE 66   ". . . in theory, but in practice": "Speech on the Repeal of the Test Laws," p. 22.

". . . exalted his nature": Edward Lascelles, *The Life of Charles James Fox*, 1936, p. 227.

PAGE 67   ". . . everything is left to accidents": *Correspondence of Edmund Burke*, vol. v, p. 177.

". . . Knight's opinion of them, but not yours": Turberville, p. 281.

". . . I must say less descriptive": Turberville, p. 196.

PAGE 68   Wordsworth assured Fox, *Early Letters of William and Dorothy Wordsworth, 1787–1805*, 1935, pp. 261–62.

Robert Bloomfield, "The Farmer's Boy," Roger Sales, *English Literary History, 1780–1830*, 1983, p. 21.

LIBERTY NOT LICENSE

PAGE 73   ". . . the French Revolution": *Critical Review*, July 1795, p. 318.

PAGE 74   ". . . neglect and accident," ". . . forcibly counteracted and suppressed": Price, 1796, pp. 34–35 note.

". . . unfit for a free country": Price, 1796, p. 378.

"dreary selfish pride," ". . . amusement and humanity": Price, 1842, p. 378.

PAGE 75   ". . . despotism of the modern improver": Price, 1842, p. 314.

". . . considerate, and connected arrangement," ". . . creating new systems": Price, 1842, p. 316.

". . . and their inhabitants, in America": Price, 1842, p. 302.

PAGE 76   "the blind, unrelenting power of system": Price, 1842, p. 305.

". . . a dread of confusion," ". . . equally favoured by the laws," ". . . any other kingdom": Price, "Thoughts on the Defense of Property," 1797, p. 14.

". . . desperate men of a great metropolis," ". . . destroys local attachments": Price, "Thoughts," p. 18.

PAGE 77   ". . . far from complete": Price, "Thoughts," p. 28.

"metaphysic fallacies," ". . . loves to soar," ". . . wise in forms," ". . . party's views": Knight, "Death of Fox," 1806.

PAGE 78   "Above the trick of Art," ". . .the Courtier's ease," "careful with lessers," "native charms": Knight, "Death of Fox," 1806.

PAGE 79   ". . . placed in proper hands": Fox, "The Speech of R.H. Charles James Fox at a General Meeting of the Electors of Westminster," July 17, 1782, p. 29.
". . . level the purity of gardens," ". . . guillotine Mr. Brown": Horace Walpole, *Correspondence*, vol. 19, pp. 338–40.
". . . the Jacobinism of taste": Frank J. Messmann, *Richard Payne Knight*, 1974, p. 83.

PAGE 80   ". . . propagating a system," ". . . improvement to prevail": Price, 1796, pp. 374–75.
". . . a state of nature": Price, 1842, p. 464.

PAGE 81   "sweet concealment": Shenstone, "A Description of the Leasowes," *The Works in Verse and Prose*.
"the ocean of life," ". . . an unextended empire," ". . . some hidden good": Joseph Craddock, *Village Memoires*, 1775, p. xi.
". . . vice and debauchery": Craddock, p. xviii.

PAGE 82   ". . . mediocrity begets respect": Craddock, p. xxi
". . . ready to introduce": Craddock, p. 144.
". . . man in a savage state," ". . . stiffness of art," ". . . despotic government," "untried, theoretical improvement": Price, 1842, p. 413.

PAGE 83   "tameness and monotony," ". . . energy and variety,"
". . .indolence and apathy," ". . . parent of anarchy": Price, 1842, pp. 442–43.
". . . merely animal instincts": *British Critic*, July, 1796, p. 29.
". . . principles of liberty and equality": Reverend John Brand, "Principles of Political Association in a State," *British Critic*, December, 1796, p. 645.

PAGE 84   ". . . may chiefly be attributed": George Mason, *An Essay on Design in Gardening*, 1768, p. 50.

". . . stripped of their ornaments": Price, 1842, p. 316.

PAGE 85   ". . . a multitude meant peace": Roy Porter, *English Society in the Eighteenth Century*, 1982, p. 187.
". . . more dreaded by monarchs than painters": Price, 1796, p. 39 note.

PAGE 86   ". . . rages in the narrow mind": Knight, *Progress*, Book II, l. 252.

PAGE 87   ". . . interest in its own": Knight, *Progress*, Book III, ll. 446–54.
". . . direct it where to rise": Knight, *Progress*, Book IV, l. 470.
". . . nor infring'd its neighbor's right": William Mason, *The English Garden*, Book II, l. 202.

PAGE 88   ". . . Its rights fair franchised": William Mason, *The English Garden*, Book III, l. 179.
". . . free and unembarrassed," ". . . the strongest impression": Archibald Alison, *Essays on the Nature and Principles of Taste*, 1812, p. 10.

PAGE 89   ". . . Turkish principles of improvement": Price, 1796, pp. 39–40 note.

ARTIFICE

PAGE 93   ". . . to what is called art": Price, 1796 p. 387.
". . . for wildness only": Price, 1842, 417.

PAGE 94   ". . . storm with icy bullets": William Mason, *The EnglishGarden*, Book III, 1. 235.

PAGE 95   ". . . materials, not their own," ". . . easy imitation": Edward Young, *Conjectures on Original Composition*, 1759, p. 12.
"patient and placable": William Mason, *The English Garden*, Book II, l. 53.

PAGE 96   ". . . pleasing to the eye": J. Hassell, *A Picturesque Guide to Bath*, 1793, pp. 8–9.
". . . the present tottering structure": Hassell, p. 10.

PAGE 97   ". . . as is consistent with comfort": Knight, p. 159.
". . . any that can be given by art": Price, 1842, p. 37.
". . . sacrificed to neatness," ". . . irrevocably destroyed": Price, 1842, pp. iv, viii.

PAGE 98   "bush-fighting mode of attack": William Marshall, *A Review of the Landscape and an Essay on the Picturesque*, 1795, p. 154.
"all libraries and picture galleries": Marshall, p. 60.
"the open display of facts": Marshall, p. 56.

PAGE 99   "furniture": Marshall, p. 256.
". . . give place to the Picturesque": Marshall, p. 74.
". . . in some degree at least, contradictory": Marshall, p. 69.
". . . suitable degree of retirement": Marshall, p. 212.
". . . to rob their masters," ". . . village with them": Marshall, p. 213.

PAGE 100   ". . . shepherds and shepherdesses": Marshall, p. 255.
". . . suspicious and suspected," ". . . aim is deception": Marshall, p. 247.
". . . husbandmen, and their attendants": Price, 1796, p. 327.
". . . but old mills": Price, p. 1796, p. 66.
". . . Of some fame," ". . . forbids to change": William Mason, *The English Garden*, Book III. l. 110.

PAGE 101   ". . . ostentasion of undivided property": Knight, p. 220, note.
". . . crowned with self-content": William Mason, *The English Garden*, Book II, l. 465.

PAGE 102   ". . . imitated in other parts": Price, 1796, p. 322.

PAGE 103   ". . . conveying our conceptions": Hassell, p. 104.
". . . the original is before us": Price, 1796, p. 5.

PAGE 104   ". . . other senses or understanding": Knight, p. 69.

PAGE 105   ". . . the use of such a study," ". . . not less so to an improver": Price, 1796, pp. 376–77.
". . . is exactly like that of speech": Price, 1842, p. 384 note.
". . . bear to each other," ". . . the works of nature": Price, 1796, pp. 8–9.

PAGE 106   "throw a reciprocal light on each other": Price, 1796, p. 11.
". . . return of consonant sounds": William Mason, *The English Garden*, Preface.
". . . is the thing it sings": William Mason, *The English Garden*, Book III, l. 79.

PAGE 107 ". . . confusing taste and feeling": *Critical Review*, November, 1805, p. 227.

". . . taste than picturesque effect": Price, 1842, p. 411.

". . . expected in garden scenery": Price, 1842, p. 416.

PAGE 108 ". . . put together on the spot": Price, 1796, p. 264 note.

". . . made by a receipt": Price, 1796, p. 29.

PAGE 109 ". . . admiration of the vulgar": Price, 1796, p. 299.

". . . drawing and composition": Knight, *Progress*, p. xii.

". . . when he has seen all": Knight, p. 448.

PAGE 110 ". . . employed, but concealed": Knight, p. 104.

". . . every discovery ourselves": Price, 1796, p. 389 note.

PAGE 111 "ravages of wealthy pride": Price, 1842, p. 400.

PAGE 112 ". . . by building a village *regularly* picturesque": Price, 1796, p. 299 note.

". . . real life are acted by Eunuchs": Price, 1842, p. 398.

". . . live without fears": Kamo-no Chomei, "Notes on a Ten-foot Square Hut," trans. Donald Keene, *Anthology of Japanese Literature*, p. 209.

PAGE 114 ". . . posts that support them," ". . . light and shadow": Price, 1842, p. 393.

". . . men of moderate means," ". . . princely fortunes": Price, 1842, p. 398.

"sweet simplicity": William Mason, *The English Garden*, Book II, l. 442.

PAGE 115 ". . . accidents around us shine": George Mason, *An Essay*, p. 31 note.

CONNECTION

PAGE 119 ". . . they have so often practised": Price, 1796, p. 351 note.

"eternal smoothness and sameness": Price, 1796, p. 16.

"mechanical common-place operation": Price, 1796, p. 40.

PAGE 120 ". . . many a common labourer": Price, 1796, p. 125.

". . . blame and ridicule": Price, 1842, p. 228.

". . . is by a system": Knight, p. 252.

". . . never descends to particles": Timothy Brownlow, *John Clare and the Picturesque Landscape*, 1983.

PAGE 121 ". . . wherever he goes": Price, 1796, p. 366 note.
"smooth, flowing and even-toned," ". . . all Mr. Brown's works," ". . . attention cannot flag": Price, 1796, p. 381–83.
"love of system": Knight, p. 74.

PAGE 122 ". . . architecture of the ancients": Knight, p. 167.
". . . method of gradual experiment": Knight, p. 448.
". . . never fall into [it]": Price, 1842, p. 218.

PAGE 123 ". . . distinct and separate": Price, 1796, p. 261.
". . . though with detached parts": Price, 1842, p. 125.
". . . ties and bonds," ". . . as well as union depends": Price, 1842, p. 179.

PAGE 124 ". . . clumped by themselves": Price, 1842, p. 179
". . . variety, effect and intricacy": Price, 1842, p. 273.
". . . delighted with that mystery": Price, 1796, pp. 262–63.
". . . the art of improvement": Price, 1796, p. 14.

PAGE 125 ". . . breadth with detail": Price, 1842, p. 127.
"inferior parts," ". . . different gradation": Price, 1842, p. 331.
"to separate, to select and combine": Price, 1796, p. 6.
". . . objects of general scenery," ". . . objects must depend": Price, 1796, p. 15.
"great author": Price, 1796, p. 62.

PAGE 126 ". . . those previously existing": Price, 1842, p. 358.
"disunited parts," ". . . majestic whole," ". . . blended": William Mason, *The English Garden*, p. 70.
". . . ideas of different people": William Gilpin, *Northern Tour*, vol. 1, p. 22.
"uses, circumstances, and situations." ". . . purposes of the whole": Price, 1842, p. 82.

PAGE 127 ". . . to existing circumstances": Price, 1842, p. 82.
". . . genuine and original character": Knight, p. 223.
Nikolaus Pevsner, *Royal Institute of British Architects Journal*, December, 1947, pp. 55–60.
". . . were most happily arranged." ". . . give way to his building":

Price, 1842, p. 368.

". . . principle and independent": Price, 1842, p. 328.

PAGE 128 ". . . on the surrounding objects," ". . . several parts," ". . . embellish each other": Price, 1842, p. 328.

". . . variety to the general outline": Price, 1796, pp. 32–33.

". . . innumerable and distinct parts": Price, 1842, p. 189.

PAGE 129 "distant mountains": Marie Lyman, "Distant Mountains," *Textile Museum Journal*, 1984, pp. 25–41.

"finely illuminate the parts," ". . . light without shadow": Price, 1796, p. 201.

PAGE 130 ". . . object of imitation": Price, 1842, p. 196.

". . . in great measure, depend": Price, 1796, p. 100.

". . . little new can occur," ". . . whole of the composition": Price, 1796, p. 142.

". . . suggest to ourselves": Price, 1842, p. 255.

PAGE 131 ". . . contradiction differ far": Jacques de Lille, *The Garden*, p. 12.

PAGE 132 ". . . knots of general harmony": Knight, *Progress*, p. 3.

PAGE 133 ". . . Multitude of Charms": Knight, *Progress*, p. 3.

". . . regulates the whole": Knight, "Death of Fox," l. 24.

". . . foresight or any plan": Richard Bentley, vol. 2, 1853, p. 7.

"Balanced interests": Knight, *Progress*, l. 167.

PAGE 134 "self-balanced rights," ". . . limits would define": Knight, *Progress*, ll. 220–21, 234.

". . . springs and weights": Knight, *Progress*, l. 240.

". . . art can ne'er restore": Knight, *Progress*, Book IV, ll. 337–50.

PAGE 135 "True wisdom," ". . . by modest doubt": Knight, *Progress*, Book IV, l. 492.

PAGE 136 "broad and dry," ". . . immediate boundaries," ". . . wanting to the other": Price, 1842, p. 310.

". . . remarkable faults": William Mason, *The English Garden*, Book I, note.

PAGE 137 ". . . not from rules": William Mason, *The English Garden*, l. 304.

"... bounds of beauty": William Mason, *The English Garden*, ll. 330–40.

"... other sense or faculty": *British Critic*, January, February, 1807, pp. 17, 173.

"... operation of the mind": *Critical Review*, November 1805, p. 226.

PAGE 137 Lord Kames, *Elements of Criticism*, 1788, Chapter 9: "Uniformity and Variety."

PAGE 138 "... in the general plan," "... his main adventure": Craddock, *Village Memoires*, p. 144.

"motion be first your care," "... an air of liberty": Jacques de Lille, *The Garden*, p. 16.

PROSPECT

PAGE 144 "... radiated outward": Lowe, *Bourgeois Perception*, p. 26.

"... solitude free of anguish": Italo Calvino, *Mr. Palomar*, p. 93.

PAGE 147 On architect and theoretician Alberti, Mark Jarzombek, *On Leon Battista Alberti*, 1989.

PAGE 148 Colin Rowe, "Character and Composition," *The Mathematics of the Ideal Villa*, 1976.

"... by an ingenious mechanic": John A. Hassell, "Views of Noblemen and Gentlemen's Seats," 1805.

PAGE 149 "... give a sombre finish": Hassell, "Views of Noblemen and Gentlemen's Seats," 1805.

Bibliography

Positioning one's own commentary in relation to a larger discourse serves two purposes: it cuts down the reverberation of speaking in an empty room where all one hears is the sound of a single voice and it tunes the argument by indicating when it is in concert and when it emerges as a solo among other voices. The following comments on selected publications relating to the Picturesque are directed to finding a distinct theme to add to those already played, not to drown them out.

The Picturesque is most immediately an art and architectural historical category filled with charming images. When Geoffrey Scott and Peter Collins review periods of architecture, the Picturesque is identified as a loose, informal look in contrast to a consistent arrangement of distinct parts. In each case the architect looks askance at a mode based so clearly on literature and painting: concrete architecture should not rely on such insubstantial sources. The Picturesque is a potentially disruptive idea to a notion of balance and order; it seems to have given up at the start any ideal of solid, resistant building.

The Picturesque, however, has also been seen as a move toward practicality or convenience in planning and siting buildings. A loosened ideal of composition gives the circumstances of land and human use an aesthetic justification to interrupt a purely geometric regularity. In the mid-twentieth century, Nikolaus Pevsner wrote and spoke in favor of a utilitarian architecture presaged by the Picturesque. In articles and books he was a champion of English common sense in the face of formal doctrines that distorted reasonable architectural arrangements. The Picturesque was pragmatic.

The charge that picturesque asymmetry was simply evidence of laziness, that the building could be set right if the architect would just try a little harder, shows how threatening relaxation is to someone operating at full bore.

The Picturesque as a visual style is less controversial when talking about paintings themselves. A love of landscape set the whole mode in motion and its appearance in pictorial images is largely unremarkable. The problem of always being aware of the need for interpretation in the face of a mode that seems to be simply a transparent presentation of a scene has been recently redefined in the world of the electronic Picturesque as Fred Ritchin's essay *In Our Own Image* demonstrates. Of course the establishment of landscape as an acceptable genre in painting in the eighteenth century was no small struggle, but once acknowledged, the delight in scenery soon reached flood tide.

When Christopher Hussey wrote *The Picturesque: Studies in a Point of View*, he took a broad prospect and by arguing beyond specific examples he tried to establish an underlying pattern discoverable in various visual forms. Bringing together the texts of the eighteenth century and selected illustrations of the principles they discussed, Hussey sought to place this salient, yet elusive mode in a developmental history of art. By seeing the Picturesque as a preparatory stage to modernism, he emphasized how the slippage between retinal stimulus and mental associations eventually led to abstract art. Such an argument is true if one views the phenomenon from a sufficiently distant position. I do not think it is less valuable for that distance, as these essays must surely indicate.

The national character of the English is often identified with the Picturesque. David Watkin's comprehensive review entitled *The English Vision* presents examples from architecture, landscape, and garden design. By assiduously collecting many familiar and not so familiar examples, he gives detailed pictures and descriptions of a hundred and fifty years of British design. As he deferentially points out, his book is more like a catalogue of things called Picturesque than it is a complex argument trying to replace Hussey.

The matter of national character is impossible to sidestep. Pevsner uses it in *The Englishness of English Art*. Watkin uses it to give importance to the Picturesque as the major British contribution to European art. Dora Wiebenson's treasure trove of examples and means of transference to France treats the style as an identifiable national orientation stemming from various sources. But it is the political associations that are the most complex, both for previous commentators and for me.

The identification of the Picturesque with liberal politics is as bald a simplification of politics as the abbreviated visual components of the Picturesque is of aesthetics. And yet the temptation to follow up this association has been indulged by others before, including Pevsner. Walter Hipple's absolute dismissal of the connection as "a mere rhetorical trick" raises the serious question, what is the point of the political metaphors in eighteenth-century texts concerning the Picturesque?

As is quite clear from reading the commentary of the time, political matters intruded in the discussion of almost everything. Such ubiquitousness could certainly suggest merely a rhetorical flourish or a willful misreading of political discourse. It is not surprising that Hipple simply calls them digressions. His treatise on the Beautiful, the Sublime, and the Picturesque is a careful exercise in making things clear. Taking various texts and subjecting them to a contemporary philosophical analysis, Hipple is not looking for ambiguity or free transportation of unlike things from one realm to another. His dismissal seems eminently warranted if one looks at I. de Wolfe's easy argument about picturesque politics as a town planning ideology in 1948. Here the political association is obviously a rhetorical tool attacking large-scale development that prevents individual things from being what they want to be. Taking the older texts more seriously than recent ones, as these essays have done, simply requires a certain distance to imagine larger compositional principles lying behind contemporary concerns.

The Picturesque can be placed in a history of the philosophical category of aesthetics and given a structural place in an
evolution of that discipline. Hipple's is a significantly traditional
effort in this kind of scholarship. A more challenging example of
contemporary rethinking of such an undertaking, although it does
not focus on the Picturesque, is Peter de Bolla's *The Discourse of the
Sublime.* De Bolla steps back beyond yet another set of frames and
subjects the eighteenth-century texts to a fascinating, if sometimes
daunting, reevaluation of how a discussion about an attitude becomes a discussion generated by that attitude, or as de Bolla puts it,
how the discourse *about* the Sublime becomes a discussion *of* the
Sublime. His identification of "the subject" is a brilliant insight and
renders any subsequent discussion vulnerable to being taken apart
frame by frame.

The Picturesque, then, has been, and has every reason for
being, considered as a visual category in art history, as a term in
philosophical discourse, as a national characteristic, and as an
embellishment of political arguments. The essays in this book are
clearly none of the above. These essays are written from yet another point of view that both takes seriously the arguments of the texts
and puts them to a purpose of present interest. As an architect, I am
on the lookout for ways to think about designing things. The
impulse to look so long and hard at the Picturesque rises from a
more general desire to compose in circumstances that seem in-
hospitable to a tradition of systematic centeredness. An interest in
texture, in irregularity more on the order of Penrose tiling, neither
random nor regularly repetitive, led me to spend time with propositions that compose in a perpetual drift between tyranny and
license.

The social implications of the Picturesque and the literary
form I take to be a correlative of it, the pastoral, have also received
important attention. The Picturesque and the pastoral have been
identified as significant ploys that either suppress social justice

under an aesthetic tyranny or upset defensive aesthetic compositions through an injection of social realism. The neoclassical pastoral taking direction from classical models and the empirical pastoral
taking contemporary social examples and nature as its sources seem
to set up a conflict between despotism and the forces of freedom.
Raymond Williams's *The Country and the City* and John Barrell's books
on the idea of landscape and its dark side depict a series of aesthetic
compositions directed at perpetuating and extending social and
political control over the land and its consumption.

Extending composition beyond its aesthetic realm can be rejected as an attack on the rights of the individual by the imposition
of control from above. It is assumed by some that the power exercised to own the land and the labor and to shape them by some
high-style disguise can redeem itself only if it is exercised by those
previously subjected to a composition. The analysis of eighteenth-
century land politics in terms of capital formation, exploitation, and
the protection of prerogatives can make the Picturesque and the
pastoral devious strategies for a ruling class.

Barrell in particular points out how the rhetoric of liberty (or
attention to smaller parts in preference to an overarching whole) is
nothing more than a clever tactic to prolong control even as it
seems to be relaxing. That, of course, is at the heart of the matter.
Whether such a move is at base a deception or an attempt to get at
a perpetually elusive condition, separates the present book from
Barrell's or Williams's.

Martin Price's essay "The Picturesque Moment," included in
From Sensibility to Romanticism, refers to several aspects of the Picturesque that these essays have pursued in some greater detail. Price's
investigation of the Picturesque in literature combines history and
composition by locating the picturesque moment between the
"centrifugal forces of dissolution and the centripetal pull of form."
He identified the preferred picturesque scenes as "those in which
form emerges only with study or is at the point of dissolution." The
peculiar status of a picturesque composition is acknowledged by the

insight that "the center of attention is displaced from the work of art as we traditionally conceive it to the large sphere in which it plays a role."

The collection of essays *The Iconography of Landscape*, edited by Denis Cosgrove and Stephen Daniels, includes several discussions of related issues. Professor Daniels's essay "The Political Iconography of Woodland in Later Georgian England" takes a close look at some political implications and is a detailed study of the period.

The perpetual controversy about whether the pastoral is nature or artifice, or versions of artifice, whether it is Virgil or Theocritus, surely indicates that something troubling is wrapped up in this matter. The Picturesque is likewise pushed from pillar to post as various interests try to enlist it in a campaign to advance an idea of freedom or of tyranny. It is not my intention to have resolved this controversy by drawing careful distinctions in hopes of getting at the truth. Neither has it been my hope to set out on an endless quest of continuous reframing so as to reduce the Picturesque to a self-induced state of mind serving only to demonstrate, once again, the limitlessness of human folly.

Ajzenstat, Janet. "Modern Mixed Government: A Liberal Defense of Inequality." *Canadian Journal of Political Science* 18, no. 1 (1985): 119–34.

Alpers, Paul J. "Convening and Convention in Pastoral Poetry." *New Literary History* 14 (1983): 277–304.

Alterton, Margaret. *Origins of Poe's Critical Theory.* New York: Russell & Russell, 1956.

Ashcraft, Richard, and M. M. Goldsmith. "Locke, Revolution Principles, and the Formation of Whig Ideology." *History Journal* (Great Britain) 26, no. 4 (1983): 772–800.

Banham, Reyner. "Revenge of the Picturesque: English Architectural Polemics, 1945–1965." In *Concerning Architecture: Essays on Architectural Writers and Writing Presented to Nikolaus Pevsner.* Edited by John Summerson. Baltimore: Penguin Books, 1968.

Barbier, Carl Paul. *William Gilpin: His Drawings, Teaching, and Theory of the Picturesque*. Oxford: Clarenden Press, 1963.

Barrell, John. *Dark Side of the Landscape: Rural Poor in English Painting, 1730–1840*. New York: Cambridge University Press, 1980

———. *The Idea of the Landscape and the Sense of Place*. New York: Cambridge University Press, 1972.

———. *Political Theory of Painting from Reynolds to Hazlitt*. New Haven: Yale University Press, 1986.

Barrell, John, and John Bull, eds. *A Book of English Pastoral Verse*. New York: Oxford University Press, 1975.

Bermingham, Ann. *Landscape and Ideology: The English Rustic Tradition, 1740–1860*. London: Thames & Hudson, 1987.

Boulton, James T., ed. *Introduction to Burke*. London: Routledge & Kegan Paul, 1958.

Bradley, James E. "Whigs and Nonconformists: 'Slumbering Radicalism' in English Politics, 1739–1789." *Eighteenth-Century Studies* 9, no. 1 (1975): 1–27.

Brand, Rev. John. "Principles of Political Associations in a State." *British Critic* 7, art. 13 (1796).

Brewer, John. "Rockingham, Burke and Whig Political Argument." *History Journal* (Great Britain) 18, no. 1 (1975): 188–201.

Briggs, Asa. *The Age of Improvement, 1783–1867*. London: Longman, 1959.

Brownlow, Timothy. *John Clare and the Picturesque Landscape*. Oxford: Clarendon Press, 1983.

Burke, Edmund. *Philosophical Enquiry into the Origin of Our Ideas of the Sublime and the Beautiful*. London, 1757.

Castell, Robert. *The Villas of the Ancients*. London, 1728.

Calvino, Italo. *If on a winter's night a traveler*. Translated by William Weaver. New York: Harcourt Brace Jovanovich, 1981.

———. *Mr. Palomar*. Translated by William Weaver. New York: Harcourt Brace Jovanovich, 1984.

Clark, H. F. "Eighteenth Century Elysiums and the Role of Associationism in the Landscape Movement." *Journal of the Warburg and Courtauld Institutes* 6 (1943): 165–89.

Clarke, Michael, and Nicholas Penny, eds. *The Arrogant Connoisseur: Richard Payne Knight, 1751–1824.* Manchester: Manchester University Press, 1982.

Clausen, W. V. *Age of Augustus.* Cambridge: Cambridge University Press, 1982.

Clemenson, Heather. *English Country Houses and Landed Estates.* Croom Helm Historical Geography Series. New York: St. Martin's Press, 1982.

Clifford, Derek. *A History of Garden Design.* New York: Praeger, 1963.

Clive, Harriet. "The Gorge at Downton." *Country Life,* 10 May 1979, p. 1441.

Collins, Peter. *Changing Ideals in Modern Architecture.* Montreal: McGill University Press, 1967.

Colvin, Howard, and John Harris, eds. *The Country Seat: Studies in the History of the British Country House Presented to Sir John Summerson on His Sixty-fifth Birthday Together with a Select Bibliography of His Published Writings.* London: Allen Lane, 1970.

Combe, William. *The Tour of Dr. Syntax: In Search of the Picturesque.* 3d rev. ed., 1813.

Congleton, James Edmund. *Theories of Pastoral Poetry in England, 1684–1798.* Gainesville: University of Florida Press, 1952.

Cooper, Anthony Ashley (3d Earl of Shaftesbury). *Characteristicks of Men, Manners, Opinions, Times.* 5th ed. corrected with the addition of a Letter Concerning the Art and Science of Design. 3 vols. London: John Darby, 1732.

Cosgrove, Denis, and Stephen Daniels, eds. *The Iconography of Landscape.* Cambridge: Cambridge University Press, 1988.

Craddock, Joseph. *Village Memoires.* London, 1775.

Deane, Phyllis. *The First Industrial Revolution.* Cambridge: Cambridge University Press, 1965.

De Bolla, Peter. *The Discourse of the Sublime.* Oxford: Basil Blackwell, 1989.

DeLille, Jacques. *The Garden: An Enquiry into the Changes of Taste in Landscape Gardening including a Defence of the Art of H. Repton, Esq.* 2d ed. London: T. Bensley, 1805.

Derry, John Wesley. *Charles James Fox*. London: B. T. Batsford, 1972.

De Selinourt, E., ed. *Letters of William and Dorothy Wordsworth*. London: Oxford University Press, 1937.

DeWolf, I. "Townscape: A Plea for an English Visual Philosophy Founded on the True Rock of Sir Uvedale Price." *Architectural Review* 106 (December 1949): 359–79.

Dickinson, H. T. *Liberty and Property: Political Ideology in Eighteenth-Century Britain*. London: Weidenfeld & Nicolson, 1977.

DuFresnoy, Charles Alphonse. *The Art of Painting*. Translated by William Mason. York, 1783.

Ellis, Harold A. "Aristocratic Influence and Electoral Independence: Two Aspects of Whig Parliamentary Reform, 1792–1832." *Journal of Modern History* 51, no. 4 (1979): viii.

Elsam, Richard. *An Essay on Rural Architecture*. London, 1803.

Empson, William. *Some Versions of Pastoral*. New York: New Directions Press, 1960.

Ettin, Andrew V. *Literature and the Pastoral*. New Haven: Yale University Press, 1984.

Feingold, Richard. *Nature and Society: Later Eighteenth-Century Use of the Pastoral and Georgic*. Brunswick, N.J.: Rutgers University Press, 1978.

Fergusson, James. *An Historical Inquiry into the True Principles of Beauty in Art More Especially with Reference to Architecture*. London: Longman Brown Green & Longmans, 1849.

Forge, J. W. Lindus. *Painshill*. Walton and Weybridge Local Historical Society, 1986.

Fosbrooke, Rev. T. D. *The Wye Tour or Gilpin on the Wye, with Picturesque Addition from Wheatley, Price, and Co. and Archaeolgical Illustrations*. 3d. ed. Ross: Printed by William Farror, 1826.

———. *The Tourist's Grammar; or Rules Relating to Scenery and Antiquities Incident to Travelers Compiled from the First Authorities, and Including an Epitome of Gilpin's Principles of the Picturesque*. London, 1826.

Fox, Charles James. *A Set of Slips containing extracts, relating to the War of American Independence, from the Letters of C. J. Fox, as published in the edition of 1815*. 1870? British Library catalog number 1850. c. 26.

———. "The Speech of the R.H. Charles James Fox Declaring His Principles Respecting the Present Crisis of Public Affairs and a Reform in the Representation of the People." London, 1792.

Fried, Michael. *Absorption and Theatricality: Painting and the Beholder in the Age of Diderot.* Berkeley: University of California Press, 1980.

Gay, Peter. *The Enlightenment: An Interpretation.* London, 1970.

Gilpin, William. *Observations Relative Chiefly to Picturesque Beauty Made in the Year 1772, on Several Parts of England; Particularly the Mountains and Lakes of Cumberland and Westmoreland.* London, 1786.

———. *Three Essays . . . To These Are Now Added Two Essays Giving an Account of the Principles and Mode in which the Author Executed His Own Drawings.* 3d ed. London: T. Cadell & W. Davies, 1808.

———. *Three Essays: On Picturesque Beauty; on Picturesque Travel; and on Sketching Landscape: to Which is Added a Poem, on Landscape Painting.* 2d ed. London: R. Blamire, 1794.

Girardin, René Louis de (Marquis). *An Essay on Landscape; or on the Means of Improving and Embellishing the Country Round our Habitations.* Translated by D. Malthus. London, 1783.

Goldsmith, Oliver. *The Citizen of the World; or Letters from a Chinese Philosopher Residing in London to His Friends in the East.* London, 1762.

———. *The Deserted Village, A Poem.* London: W. Griffin, 1770.

———. *The Life of Richard Nash of Bath, Esq.* London, 1762.

Hassell, John A. *A Picturesque Guide to Bath, Bristol Hot-Wells, the River Avon, and the Adjacent Country.* London, 1793.

———. *Views of Noblemen and Gentlemen's Seats, Antiquities, and Remarkable Buildings in the Counties Adjoining London.* London, 1804–5.

Hill, B.W. "Fox and Burke: The Whig Party and the Question of Principles, 1784–1789." *English History Review* 89 (1974): 1–24.

Hipple, Walter J., Jr. *The Beautiful, the Sublime, and the Picturesque in Eighteenth-Century British Aesthetic Theory.* Carbondale, Ill.: Southern Illinois University Press, 1957.

Hobhouse, Christopher. *Fox.* London: Constable & Co., 1934.

Home, Henry (Lord Kames). *Elements of Criticism.* 6th ed. Edinburgh, 1785.

Hughes, Peter, and David Williams, eds. *The Varied Pattern: Studies in the Eighteenth Century*. Toronto: A. M. Hakkert, 1971.

Hunt, John Dixon. *Garden and Grove*. Princeton: Princeton University Press, 1986.

———. *William Gilpin: A Dialogue upon the Gardens of the Right Honorable The Lord Viscount Cobham at Stow in Buckinghamshire, 1748*. Reprint: Bedford College, University of London.

Hunt, John Dixon, and Peter Willis, eds. *The Genius of the Place*. New York: Harper & Row, 1975.

Hussey, Christopher. *The Picturesque: Studies in a Point of View*. London: F. Cass, 1927.

Inglis-Jones, Elisabeth. "The Knights of Downton Castle": Parts 1 and 2. *National Library of Wales Journal* 15, nos. 3, 4 (1968).

Ireland, Samuel. *Picturesque View on the River Wye*. London, 1797.

Jacques, David. *Georgian Gardens: The Reign of Nature*. London: B. T. Batsford, 1983.

Johnson, D. T. "Charles James Fox: From Government to Opposition 1771–1774." *English History Review* 89 (1974): 750–84.

Kamo-no Chomei. "Notes on a Ten Foot Square Hut" Translated by Donald Keene, *Anthology of Japanese Literature*. New York: Grove Press, 1955.

Kermode, Frank, ed. *English Pastoral Poetry*. New York: W. W. Norton & Co., 1952. Norton Library, 1972.

———. *Introduction to The Tempest*. Arden Shakespeare. London: Methuen, 1964.

Kliger, Samuel. "Whig Aesthetics: A Phase of Eighteenth-Century Taste." *Journal of English Literary History* 16 (1949): 135–50.

Knight, Richard Payne. *An Analytical Inquiry into the Principles of Taste*. 4th ed. London: T. Payne, 1808.

———. *Expedition into Sicily*. Claudia Stumpf, ed. London: British Museum Publications, 1986.

———. *The Landscape, A Didactic Poem in Three Books*. London: 1794.

———. "The Life of Sir Joshua Reynolds by James Northcote." *Edinburgh Review*, 1814, pp. 263–92.

——. *Progress of a Civil Society.* London, 1796.

——. "Review of Civil Society." *British Critic,* 1796, pp. 24–32.

Kramnick, Isaac. *Bolingbroke and His Circle: The Politics of Nostalgia in the Age of Walpole.* Cambridge, Mass.: Harvard University Press, 1968.

Kriegel, Abraham D. "Liberty and Whiggery in Early Nineteenth-Century England." *Journal of Modern History* 52, no. 2 (1980): 253–78.

Lascelles, Edward. *The Life of Charles James Fox.* London: Oxford University Press, 1936.

Lauder, Sir Thomas Dick. *Sir Uvedale Price on the Picturesque, With an Essay on the Origin of Taste.* Edinburgh, 1842.

Lincoln, Eleanor Terry, ed. *Pastoral and Romance: Modern Essays in Criticism.* Englewood Cliffs, N.J.: Prentice-Hall, 1969.

Lipking, Lawrence. *The Ordering of the Arts in Eighteenth-Century England.* Princeton: Princeton University Press, 1970.

Lipscomb, George. *Journey into South Wales.* London: Longman, 1802.

Lochhead, Ian J. *The Spectator and the Landscape in the Art Criticism of Diderot and His Contemporaries.* Ann Arbor, Mich.: UMI Research Press.

Lowe, Donald. *History of Bourgeois Perception.* Chicago: University of Chicago Press, 1982.

Lyman, Marie. " 'Distant Mountains': The Influence of Funzo-e on the Tradition of Buddhist Clerical Robes in Japan." *Textile Museum Journal* 23 (1984): 25–41.

Mack, Maynard. *The Garden and the City: Retirement and Politics in the Later Poetry of Pope, 1731–1743.* Toronto: University of Toronto Press, 1969.

McKay, A. G. *Houses, Villas, and Palaces in the Roman World.* London: Thames & Hudson, 1975.

McKenzie, Gordon. *Critical Responses: A Study of the Psychological Current in Later Eighteenth-Century Criticism.* Berkeley: University of California Press, 1949.

Malins, Edward Greenway. *English Landscaping and Literature, 1660-1840.* London: Oxford University Press, 1966.

Marinelli, Peter V. *Pastoral.* London: Methuen & Co., 1971.

Marshall, William. *A Review of The Landscape, a Didactic Poem: Also of an Essay on the Picturesque [by Sir Uvedale Price] with Remarks on Rural Ornament by the Author of "Planting and Ornamental Gardening, a Practical Treatise."* London, 1795.

Mason, George. *An Essay on Design in Gardening.* London: Printed for Benjamin White, 1768.

Mason, William. *The English Garden: A Poem in Four Books.* York, London: 1777–81.

Matthews, John. *A Sketch from The Landscape, a Didactic Poem Addressed to Richard Payne Knight with Notes, Illustrations and a Postscript.* London, 1794. Or William Mason according to George W. Johnson.

Messmann, Frank J. *Richard Payne Knight: The Twilight of Virtuosity.* The Hague: Mouton, 1974.

Mingay, G. E. *English Landed Society in the Eighteenth Century.* London: Routledge & Kegan Paul, 1963.

Mitchell, Leslie George. *Charles James Fox and the Disintegration of the Whig Party, 1782–1794.* London: Oxford University Press, 1971.

Mitford, William. *Principles of Design in Architecture Traced in Observations on Buildings.* 2d. ed. London, 1824.

Monk, Samuel. *The Sublime.* (1935) Ann Arbor, Mich.: UMI Research Press, 1962.

Nares, Gordon. "Painshill Surrey." *Country Life* 123 (1958):18–21, 62–65.

Nichols, J., ed. *The Gentleman's Magazine and Historical Chronicle,* 1754, pp. 269–70; 1757, pp. 216–18; 1795, p. 270; 1797, pp. 473–74; 1806, p. 132.

O'Gorman, Frank. *The Rise in Party in England: The Rockingham Whigs, 1760–1782.* London: Allen & Unwin, 1975.

———. *The Whig Party and the French Revolution.* London: Macmillan, 1967.

Pace, Clair. "Strong Contraries . . . Happy Discord: Stowe Eighteenth-Century Discussions About Landscape." *Journal of the History of Ideas,* 1979, pp. 141–55.

Parreaux, André; Michele Plaisanet, Jacques Carré, Marie Thérèse

Fombonne, and Jacques Michon. *Jardin et paysages; le style anglais.* Villeneuve-d'Ascq: Université de Lille, 1977.

Pevsner, Nikolaus. "C-20 Picturesque." *Architectural Review* 115 (1954): 227–29.

———. *The Englishness of English Art: An Expanded and Annotated Version of the Reith Lectures Broadcast in October and November, 1955.* Harmondsworth: Penguin Books, 1964.

———. "From Mannerism to Romanticism." *Studies in Art, Architecture, and Design.*Vol. 1. New York: Walker & Co., 1968.

———. "Genesis of the Picturesque." *Architectural Review* 46 (November 1944): 46.

———. "Richard Payne Knight." *Art Bulletin* 31 (1949): 292–320.

———. "Roehampton: LCC Housing and the Picturesque Tradition." *Architectural Review,* July 1959, pp. 21–35.

Plumb, J. H. *Growth of Political Stability in England.* London: Macmillan, 1967.

Poggioli, Renato. *The Oaten Flute: Essays on Pastoral Poetry and the Pastoral Ideal.* Cambridge, Mass.: Harvard University Press, 1975.

Pope, Alexander. "On Gardens." *Guardian,* 29 September 1713.

———. *An Epistle to the Right Honorable Richard Earl of Burlington.* London: P. L. Gilliver, 1731.

Porter, Roy. *English Society in the Eighteenth Century.* Pelican Social History of Britain. New York: Penguin Books, 1982.

Potter, Robert. *Observation on the Poor Laws, on the Present State of the Poor, and on Houses of Industry.* London, 1775.

Price, Martin. "The Picturesque Moment." In *From Sensibility to Romanticism: Essays Presented to Frederick A. Pottle.* Edited by Frederick W. Hilles and Harold Bloom. New York: Oxford University Press, 1965.

Price, Uvedale. *An Essay on the Picturesque as Compared with the Sublime and the Beautiful, and on the Use of Studying Pictures for the Purpose of Improving Real Landscape.* 2d ed. Hereford, 1798.

———. *Thoughts on the Defence of Property.* Hereford, 1797.

Puttenham, George. "Arte of English Poesie" (1589), *Elizabethan Critical Essays*. Edited byG. G. Smith. Oxford: Oxford University Press, 1904.

Quaintance, Richard E. "Walpole's Whig Interpretation of Landscaping History." *Studies in Eighteenth-Century Culture* 9 (1979): 285–300.

Reid, Thomas. *An Inquiry into the Human Mind on the Principles of Common Sense*. Glasgow: University of Glasgow, 1817.

Repton, Humphrey. *A Letter to Uvedale Price, Esq.* London, 1794.

———. *An Inquiry into the Changes of Taste in Landscape Gardening*. London, 1806.

Richards, Judith, Lotte Mulligan, and John Graham. " 'Property' and 'People': Political Usages of Locke and Some Contemporaries." *Journal of the History of Ideas* 42, no. 1 (1981): 29–51.

Robbins, Caroline. *Eighteenth-Century Commonwealthman*. Cambridge, Mass: Harvard University Press, 1961.

Robinson, Peter Frederick. *Designs for Farm Buildings*. London, 1830.

———. *Village Architecture: Being a Series of Designs Illustrative of the Observations in the Essay on the Picturesque by Sir Uvedale Price: and as a Supplement to a Work on Rural Architecture*. London, 1830.

Rosenblum, Robert. *Transformations in Late Eighteenth Century Art*. Princeton: Princeton University Press, 1967.

Rosenmeyer, Thomas G. *The Green Cabinet: Theocritus and the European Pastoral Lyric*. Berkeley: University of California Press, 1969.

Rothstein, Eric. "Ideal Presence and the Non-Finite in Eighteenth-Century Aesthetics." *Eighteenth-Century Studies* 9 (1975): 307–32.

Rowe, Colin. "Character and Composition; Or, Some Vicissitudes of Architectural Vocabulary in the Nineteenth Century." *The Mathematics of the Ideal Villa and Other Essays*. Cambridge, Mass.: MIT Press, 1976.

Russell, John (Lord). *Memorials and Correspondence of Charles James Fox*. London, 1853.

Sales, Roger. *English Literature in History, 1780–1830: Pastoral and Politics*. London: Hutchinson & Co., 1983.

Sambrook, James. *English Pastoral Poetry*. Boston: Twayne Publishers, 1983.

Scott, Geoffrey. *The Architecture of Humanism*. 2d ed. New York: Charles Scribner's Sons, 1924.

Segal, Charles. *Poetry and Myth in Ancient Pastoral: Essays on Theocritus and Virgil*. Princeton: Princeton University Press, 1981.

Shaw, Stebbing. *A Tour in 1787 from London to the Western Highlands of Scotland including Excursions to the Lakes of Westmoreland and Cumberland*. London, 1788.

——. *A Tour to the West of England in 1788*. London: Robson & Clarke, 1789.

Shearer, E. A. "Wordsworth and Coleridge: Marginalia in Richard Payne Knight's Inquiry in the Principles of Taste." *Huntington Quarterly* 1 (1937): 63–94.

Shenstone, William. *The Works in Verse and Prose of William Shenstone, Esq., Most of Which Were Never Before Printed*. Edited by R. Dodsley. 3 vols. London: R. & J. Dodsley, 1765.

Smith, John Thomas (Engraver of the Antiquities of London). *Remarks on Rural Scenery with Twenty Etchings of Cottages from Nature and Some Observations and Precepts Relative to the Picturesque*. London, 1797.

Snell, Bruno. *The Discovery of the Mind*. Translated by T. G. Rosenmeyer. Cambridge, Mass.: Harvard University Press, 1953.

Starobinski, Jean. *The Invention of Liberty*. Translated from the French by Bernard C. Swift. Geneva: Skira, 1964.

Stewart, Dugald. *Philosophical Essays*. Edinburgh, 1810.

Symes, Michael. "Charles Hamilton's Plantings at Painshill." *Garden History* 11, no. 2.

Tasso, Torquato. *Jerusalem Delivered*. Translated and edited by Ralph Nash. Detroit: Wayne State University Press, 1987.

Taylor, Nicholas. *The Village in the City*. London: Temple Smith, 1973.

Temple, Sir William. "Upon the Garden of Epicurus; or Of Gardening in the Year 1685." In *Miscellanea*, Part 2. London, 1720.

Templeman, William Darby. *The Life and Work of William Gilpin (1724–1804): Master of the Picturesque and Vicar of Boldre*. Illinois Studies in Language and Literature, vol. 24, nos. 3–4. Urbana, Ill.: University of Illinois Press, 1939.

Thompson, F. M. L., ed. *The Rise of Suburbia*. Leicester, Leicestershire: Leicester University Press, 1982.

Thomson, James. *Liberty*. London: A. Millar, 1735–36.

Tipping, H. Avery. "Downton Castle." *Country Life*, 14 July 1917, pp. 36–42.

Turberville, A. S. *A History of Welbeck Abbey and Its Owners*, Vol. 2: 1755–1875. London: Faber & Faber, 1934.

Vandervell, Anthony, and Charles Coles. *Game and the English Landscape*. New York: Viking Press, 1980.

Walpole, Horace. *Correspondence*. New Haven and London: Yale University Press, 1937–74.

Watkin, David. *The English Vision*. London: John Murray, 1982.

Watson, J. R. *Picturesque Landscape and English Romantic Poetry*. London: Hutchinson Educational, 1970.

Watts, William. *The Seats of the Nobility and Gentry*. London, 1779–86.

Wayne, Don. *Penshurst: The Semiotics of Place and the Poetics of History*. Madison: University of Wisconsin Press, 1984.

Weaver, Bruce J. "Debate and the Destruction of Friendship: An Analysis of Fox and Burke on the French Revolution." *Quarterly Journal of Speech* 61, no. 1 (1981): 57–63.

Whatley, Thomas. *Observations on Modern Gardening, Illustrated by Descriptions*. London, 1770.

White, Christopher. *English Landscape, 1630–1850: Drawings, Prints, and Books*. Paul Mellon Collection. London: Yale Center for the British Arts, 1977.

Whitney, Lois. *Primitivism and the Idea of Progress in English Popular Literature of the Eighteenth Century*. Baltimore: Johns Hopkins University Press, 1934.

Wiebenson, Dora. *The Picturesque Garden in France*. Princeton: Princeton University Press, 1978.

Williams, Raymond. *The Country and the City*. New York: Oxford University Press, 1973.

Willis, Peter, ed. *Essays on the History of the English Landscape Garden in Memory of H. F. Clark*. London, 1974.

Willis, Richard. "'An Handful of Violent People': The Nature of the Foxite Opposition, 1794–1801." *Albion* 8, no. 3 (1976): 236–54.

Wittkower, Rudolf. "Imitation, Eclecticism and Genius." *Aspects of the Eighteenth Century*. Edited by Earl Wasserman. Baltimore: Johns Hopkins University Press, 1965.

——. *Palladio and English Palladianism*. London: Thames & Hudson, 1974.

Wolf, Janet. *The Social Production of Art*. New York: St. Martin's Press, 1981.

Wood, John. *A Series of Plans for Cottages or Habitations of the Labourer*. London: J. & J. Taylor, 1781.

Woodbridge, Kenneth. *Landscape and Antiquity: Aspects of English Culture at Stourhead, 1718–1838*. London: Clarendon Press, 1970.

Woodforde, John. *The Truth about Cottages*. London: Routledge & Kegan Paul, 1969.

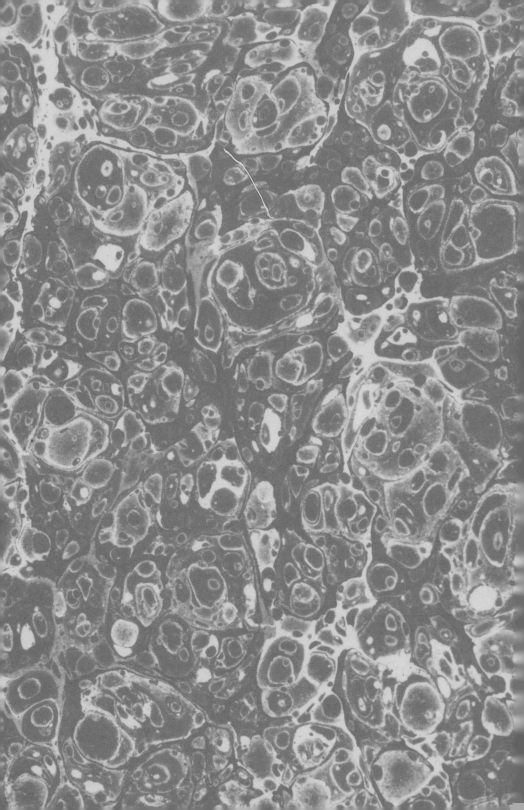